ABOUT THE AUTHORS

Joanne Elphinston B.Phty MA MCSP is an Australian performance consultant, physiotherapist and lecturer with special interests in motor control, rehabilitation and performance enhancement in sport and the performing arts. She has practised in Australia, the USA and Great Britain, and works with professional dancers, musicians, national sporting bodies and elite athletes in a wide variety of sports including weight lifting, martial arts, athletics, swimming, golf and racquet sports. Joanne has been developing applications for the Swiss Ball since 1991, and lectures extensively on applied stability concepts.

Paul Pook BA (Hons) MA is strength and conditioning coach for NEC Harlequins RFC and ʰ ʳ worked with elite athletes in a wide variety of sports. He is ˌ ₂₀₁₅ ₔ Conditioning for Rugby and edits www.fitnes‾ ᵇʸ fitness ᵂ ᵇ site.

The training programme in this manual has been devised with safety as its priority. The authors advocate careful, responsible use of the ball. The Safety Check and Medical History sections are provided as a guide but in no way replace the supervision of a trained medical professional. The authors and publisher cannot be held liable for injuries sustained during the Core Workout, or by misuse or misunderstanding associated with the material herein.

Enquiries to:-

Paul T Pook - Fitness 4 Sport LLP
Tel: 01252 816666   www.fitness4rugby.com
e-mail: paul@fitness4rugby.com

Joanne Elphinston - Elphinston Human Performance
e-mail: jelphinston@yahoo.com

The concept of core stability and muscle balance is increasingly being recognised as fundamental in good training practice, both for the prevention of injury and to optimise physical performance. However, many sportspeople and trainers have difficulty finding effective and motivating methods to integrate core stability training into their programmes. It was with this in mind that we produced The Core Workout, which is based on our experiences in training a wide variety of elite athletes and sportspeople in core stability and movement efficiency.

Initially, we began to work together with the purpose of combining our different professional backgrounds of physiotherapy and sport science, aiming to develop safe and effective training strategies for performance enhancement. An integral part of this approach has been Swiss Ball training, as we have found over time that we can tailor a core stability programme from the very basic to the very advanced, that athlete compliance is excellent because the ball is challenging and fun to work with, and that it allows us many alternatives if an athlete is injured. We have also found the ball to be particularly useful in team training and group situations, which has led to the original exercises presented in the Double Trouble section of this manual.

The Core Workout was originally a record of our ideas and development as our applications to different sporting needs expanded, but over time the demand from various sporting bodies and individual sportspeople has increased for a text from which they can work and progress. There are several books on the market dealing with low level exercise, but few which address stability training at the advanced level required by an athlete, so this manual is intentionally pitched to address this need. The ball's versatility in a rehabilitation setting is limitless, however it is not within the scope of this manual to adequately address this topic, despite the strong temptation to do so!

As a final note, the Swiss Ball is a versatile tool for training and is currently being used at very high levels for training in a wide range of sports. We have international sprinters, rugby players, archers, surfers, golfers and martial artists training on balls to name but a few, and combined with a better understanding of their own body movement and function, they are experiencing excellent results. We encourage you to use the ball with a bit of imagination and creativity, and hope that equipped with the principles which are introduced here, you will find ways to make it a relevant and valuable part of your training.

CONTENTS

CORE STABILITY FOR SPORT AND CONDITIONING

Strength, speed, flexibility and agility are among the fitness parameters commonly trained to make you effective in sport. The type of sport or the position you play will affect the relative balance of these qualities, but whether it be in a team sport or downhill skiing, you are ultimately aiming for a balance which will lead to physical control and optimal performance.

Training often focuses on obvious, easily visible muscle groups in the arms and legs. While the relationship between these muscles and the movements of the limbs is readily accepted, eg. hamstring muscles and the knee bending movement, what is overlooked is an understanding that these muscles of the limbs depend on a solid foundation to pull from for their effectiveness. Training core stability develops this foundation.

What is Core Stability?

Core stability provides central body control, and allows you to generate power by maximising the efficiency of your muscular effort. **It is the ability of your trunk to support the effort and forces from your arms and legs, so that muscles and joints can perform in their safest, strongest and most effective positions.**

Your core is not just your back, but also the pelvic and shoulder girdles, which are responsible for transferring the forces of your arms and legs to your spine. The shoulder girdle is made up of your collar bones and your shoulder blades, and provides an anchor for your arm movements through muscular attachments to your midback. The pelvic girdle functions in a similar manner, with the abdominal and gluteal muscles working to maintain its position relative to the spine. This allows the pelvis to provide a stable base for your legs to pull from.

If the wrong muscles are activated to transfer the forces from your limbs through these girdles to your spine, or if the appropriate muscles work but are relatively weak, the body will try to find a way to compensate. It does this by adjusting other parts of the body into positions that are not necessarily ideal for the demands of the movement. When this occurs, you lose efficiency, and this translates into a loss of power. It can also make you vulnerable to injuries such as shoulder tendonitis or lower back pain.

The muscles responsible for optimal force transfer between the limbs and the spine, i.e. those that stabilise your central body, or *core*, are therefore essential for optimal body functioning. You cannot avoid this force transfer, but you can improve the way in which it happens, to make it safer and more efficient. It doesn't matter how much weight training you do on your arms and legs: **you can only be as strong as your weakest link, and if that link is your *core* stability, you need to train for it specifically.**

How can Core Stability improve my performance?

By training specifically for core stability, you gain a number of benefits:

- more efficient use of muscle power, as less effort is lost in compensatory movements in the trunk.
- decreased injury risk, as forces are sent to the appropriate part of the body to control them.
- increased ability to change direction, as body momentum is controlled
- greater capacity for speed generation
- improved balance and muscular coordination
- improved posture

How do I train for core stability?

You need to train specifically for the tasks required. In other words, you train the stabilising muscles to hold the trunk and girdles steady while you introduce resistance from the arms, legs, or gravity. For example, the abdominal muscles, key stabilisers, are often only trained with sit-ups, and this trunk curling movement does not necessarily relate to the abdominals' role in supporting your trunk while running, swinging a golf club, or changing direction quickly. By performing sit-ups you would be training the abdominals as *mobilisers*, muscles which create motion, as opposed to training the muscles as *stabilisers*, those which support and hold against the forces of the moving limbs.

Bodies also need to be trained to work effectively in multiple planes of movement. Many of the exercises we do focus on one plane at a time, for example bench pressing on a machine, but this will not necessarily transfer onto the playing field. The body in sport constantly moves through combinations of joint rotation, often incorporating the trunk and limbs simultaneously. This rotation is necessary for full functional range of motion, and also for "winding up" the muscles so that they temporarily store energy for movement, something like twisting up a rubber band and then seeing the quick movement it produces when released.

The core stabilising muscles are responsible for controlling these rotatory forces, however this control does not develop by repeatedly performing movements in one plane, especially when fully supported. Exercising on an unstable base like the exercise ball helps to stimulate multidirectional control, and helps to "wake up" the core stabilisers.

Core stability and lower back pain

Recent research has shown that the muscles responsible for supporting the lower back are the very muscles which stop working effectively in the presence of pain. Whether you are involved in an athletic pursuit or not, these muscles are necessary to control movement of the trunk and limbs, and limit excessive stress on the spine.

The principles outlined for sports performance therefore also apply in the case of back pain. Development of a strong, stable trunk or 'core' is essential to recover from a back injury, even if you just want to return to everyday tasks. Control of movement in many planes is part of normal activity, and training the body to activate the stabilising muscles and then to respond to an unstable surface such as the ball can contribute to this process.

At first, activating the stabilisers takes a lot of 'brain work' - you have to develop a relationship with muscles that you may not have consciously tried to work before. This isn't always easy! Developing core stability will require mental focus to begin with, but gradually over time these muscles will begin to activate automatically and appropriately for you.

The Core Muscles

Abdominals

It comes as a surprise to most people that the abdominals are not just one muscle, but are in fact made up of the rectus abdominis, internal and external obliques, and transversus abdominis muscles. These muscles all have a different action and function. Athletes spend a great deal of time training one or two muscles, once again with standard sit-ups and perhaps sit-ups with a twist, but never access the most important abdominal muscles of all - the transversus abdominis, or "trans abs". These muscles wrap around the entire trunk wall, inserting into the fascia which covers the spine, and they play a primary role in keeping the lumbar spine and pelvis stable during movement.

ABDOMINAL WALL - NOTE THAT TRANSVERSUS ABDOMINIS WRAPS AROUND THE TRUNK TO SUPPORT THE LUMBAR SPINE.

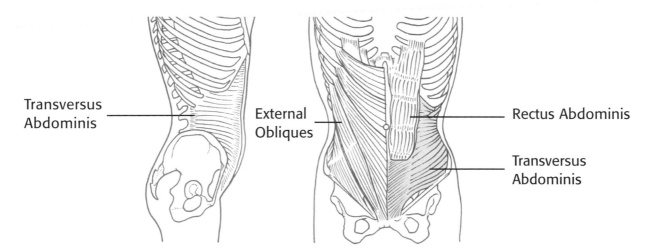

Transversus Abdominis

External Obliques

Rectus Abdominis

Transversus Abdominis

Gluteals

The muscles around your hip and bottom are not just for sitting on - these muscles are extremely important power *generators*. The gluteus maximus (or "glute max") is activated whenever the hip must move between bending and straightening. This means it has a key role in **speed** (think of the prominent buttocks which you see on top sprinters), **lifting** whether it be in a lineout or a dead lift, jumping forward or upward, **controlling** a landing, or even contributing to **balance** as a lawn bowler steps forward!

If you are involved in a propulsive sport such as netball, rugby or sprinting, think of glute max as an "engine" which drives your body forward and upward. If your sport is requires accuracy and defined movements, the glutes increase control and contribute to a stable base to shoot, swing, kick or balance from. Many of our clients, regardless of their sport, are too weak in their glutes to adequately control their hip, knee or back, and not only risk injury but are unable to perform to their potential.

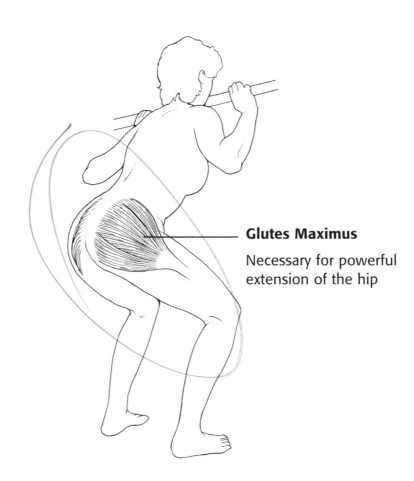

Glutes Maximus

Necessary for powerful extension of the hip

Other muscles of this region, such as gluteus medius, are responsible for side to side stability of the pelvis as well as sideways leg movement. Without this muscle functioning properly, you cannot stand on one leg without your pelvis tipping, leading to compensatory side bending of your spine and excess stress to the lower back or other parts of the pelvis, once again decreasing efficiency and risking injury.

HIP ABDUCTOR FUNCTION

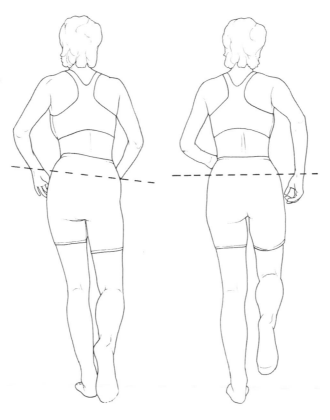

Inadequate Stability

If Glutes Medius is weak, the pelvis may tip when weight bearing on that side

Adequate Stability

With better hip abductor function, the pelvis remains level on weight bearing

The gluteals are also critical in the support of the lower back, and are often found to be weak and under-active in individuals with lower back pain. When this occurs, you may tend to overuse your back and knees to make up for the weakness, and even everyday activities such as climbing stairs and getting out of a chair can become altered to compensate.

There are numerous smaller muscles in the hip region which have important roles to play in stability, and throughout the Core Workout they will be activated to assist the larger muscles to control your hip and knee position. The gluteals, however, need particular attention, as weakness in these muscles is strongly correlated with back, knee and groin injuries.

Upper Body Stability

In the upper body, the core muscles are just as important. Just as the abdominals and gluteals contribute to and help control lower limb and back movement, another set of muscles performs the same role for the upper limb. In order for you to be able to move your arm, the muscles responsible for the movement must have a stable base to pull from. This base is your shoulder blade, or scapula. However, to fulfill this role, the scapula must be fixed to the trunk in some way, otherwise the force will be lost from your arm movement.

The muscles which are responsible for this scapular control are the upper and lower trapezius, which attach to the skull and larger bones of the lower mid-back, and the serratus anterior, which attaches to the ribs. These attachments give a relatively large surface area to support arm forces, and combine to angulate the scapula upwards, giving the "ball" of the ball and socket joint of the shoulder room to rotate in the movement of lifting the arm.

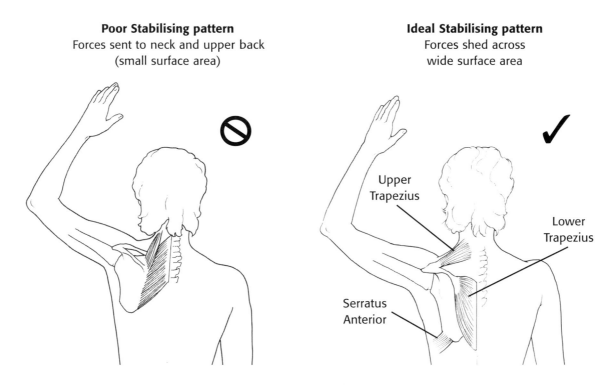

Poor Stabilising pattern
Forces sent to neck and upper back
(small surface area)

Ideal Stabilising pattern
Forces shed across
wide surface area

Upper Trapezius

Lower Trapezius

Serratus Anterior

Often, however, we see athletes who do not use this pattern to achieve arm movement. Instead of staying flat on the rib cage, their scapulae lift off or "wing", and neck and upper back muscles pull the scapula upwards. This has two effects. The first is that arm power decreases, as the forces are sent to smaller, weaker areas such as the neck. The second is that injury risk is increased, both in the joints of the neck, as well as the tendons of the shoulder. If the scapula does not angulate upwards, there is a risk that the tendons of your shoulder will be compressed, leading to painful tendonitis.

Once the scapula is well positioned to provide a good "socket" angle, the muscles of the rotator cuff help to control the movement of the "ball" of the shoulder joint. These muscles have a critical role to play, making sure that the rolling and sliding motion of normal shoulder movement does not deviate forwards or upwards within the socket. Core Workout exercises involving the arms demand a great deal of stabilising muscle activity around the shoulder and if you maintain good body position, Swiss Ball training can stimulate and strengthen the rotator cuff.

ROTATOR CUFF

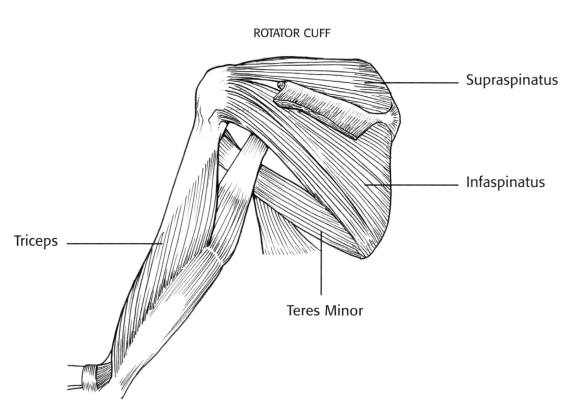

Supraspinatus

Infaspinatus

Triceps

Teres Minor

Summary

Training for athletic performance has become considerably more sophisticated in recent years. For both athletes and sports professionals, the time has passed when "doing what we've always done" is acceptable, just as using exercises and techniques without understanding how or why they are supposed to work is not good practice. Increasingly, a knowledge of how the body functions, along with a good grasp of the specific physical and psychological demands of the sport is necessary to really achieve results and avoid injury over time.

The principles which shape a programme for core stability are :

Understand the demands of your sport. Training may focus on a selection of characteristics, but perhaps not consider the interplay between them. Ask yourself what the sport breaks down into for the individual player or athlete e.g. Linear speed, rapid change of direction, upward or forward explosive power, rotational control, blocking the forces of other players, ability to stop suddenly, ability to balance in a variety of body positions , ability to control ballistic actions of the upper and lower limbs etc. If the sport requires a complex movement, such as in gymnastics or power lifting, make sure that you have a clear understanding of how such a movement is achieved.

Develop an understanding of basic anatomy and muscle actions. If you understand how your body works, it will subtly alter how you perform your movements, and help to focus your mind on what you are doing. For example, an athlete with a poor concept of muscle action and inadequate training objectives may decide to perform a bicep curl to increase bicep strength, but fails to focus on which muscles are responsible for movement, and which muscles are necessary for support. He or she simply aims to "get the weight up", which leads to the use of momentum (swinging) combined with back motion to lift the weight. The whole body starts to move, instead of what should be a simple elbow bending movement using concentrated bicep muscle effort, founded on a stabilised shoulder blade and trunk for correct support. The result of this lack of understanding is a relatively poor outcome for the effort and time spent, and a further safety risk.

Train muscles specifically for their role in your sport. If the muscle should stabilise, train it for that role, both in isolation and whenever you train the mobilising muscles which it should support. Also remember that in sport, balance and quick muscle reactions in multiple planes are required, and that these features should be built upon a foundation of core stability.

THE SWISS BALL

Although the Swiss Ball has been around since the 1930's, its potential for high level exercise has not been widely recognised until recently. The major advantage of Swiss Ball training is that it provides an unstable support surface, which stimulates the body's stabilising mechanisms. This allows you to train the function of the muscles and not just their strength.

The Swiss Ball is extremely versatile, and can be used for a variety of purposes. For example, as a weights bench, it can alter your angle of effort, and demand the support of your stabilising muscles to increase the effectiveness and functional carry over of your exercise.

Equipment Guidelines

Do not inflate your ball over the maximum prescribed diameter. The correct diameter is the same as the size indicated on the ball. This is the **maximum** diameter of the ball.

To inflate:

1. Mark the indicated height of the ball on a wall.

2. Remove the plug from the ball and inflate with a manual pump or air compressor. Do not over inflate.

3. Measure the ball against the marked indicator on the wall.

   To deflate your Swiss ball, remove the plug carefully by exerting a pulling pressure while moving the plug back and forth.

Basic Safety

1. Use only on a safe level ground

2. Wear shoes with non-slip soles

3. Avoid contact with sharp objects or sources of heat

4. Make sure that your practice space is clear and unobstructed

5. Do not use near stairs

6. Small parts such as the plugs may be easily swallowed, so care should be taken with small children

To perform The Core Workout safely and for optimal results, there are several basic principles that must be understood.

Neutral Alignment

Neutral alignment allows the joints and muscles to perform at their best with the least risk of injury. This neutral alignment must be maintained throughout the movements in The Core Workout. Your key areas of focus are the neck, shoulder blades and pelvis. Deviations from neutral not only decrease your body's efficiency, but increase your potential for injury and body pain

To find your neutral position, stand relaxed, and then **draw yourself up from the back of your head**, lengthening your spine. Your posture should change automatically in a number of ways. Notice that your chin may lower slightly and the back of your neck may flatten slightly. Your shoulders should be relaxed down away from your ears, and not too far forward. Your pelvis should be level under your shoulders, and your stomach slightly flattened.

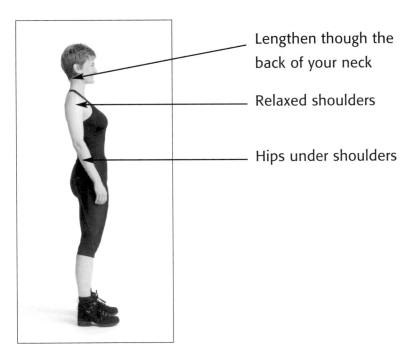

Lengthen though the back of your neck

Relaxed shoulders

Hips under shoulders

POOR POSTURE   IMPROVED POSTURE

These positions should be maintained whether you are standing, sitting, on your back

LYING SUPINE ON THE BALL

or on your front...

LYING PRONE ON THE BALL

Stomach Scooping

A key movement to master is **stomach scooping**. Drawing the very lower part of your belly back and slightly up as if 'scooping it' towards your spine activates your transversus abdominis muscles, otherwise known as the 'trans abs.' This activation stabilises your trunk and allows you to generate more power from your arms and legs.

To finds your trans abs, place your hand on your lower belly and draw yourself up from the back of your head as outlined in 'neutral alignment.' You will find that this action will automatically bring the stomach in, allowing the body to lengthen and narrow through the waist area. Now slowly raise an arm above your head, keeping the feeling of being long, straight and narrow through the waist, and you should find that the stomach draws in a little more in order to prevent your spine from sagging forward. Your trans abs allow your limbs to move while keeping the spine in a safe, efficient position.

The concept of *lengthening and narrowing* is very important to sustain, particularly as the exercises become more challenging. It is tempting to use other muscles which give an impression of abdominal tautness, but which pull the rib cage down towards the pubic bone. Instead, keep a consistent distance between your pubic bone and breast bone - if you feel as if you are 'compressing' or 'gripping' your middle, you are not using your trans abs.

Getting in touch with your trans abs may be difficult, and different ways of accessing them may be necessary at first. Here are several other methods for further developing your awareness of trans abs.

1 Begin by lying on your back with your knees bent. Breathe out fully, and before breathing in, draw the lower stomach back towards the spine, as if scooping the area below the belly button back and slightly upwards. Sustain this contraction, and proceed with breathing.

If you have difficulty breathing, place your hands on your lower ribs, and make sure that as you breathe in, your ribs expand under your hands, and as you breathe out, that your ribs ease back in again. You should be able to do this while maintaining the 'scooping' feeling in your lower abdominals.

2 Lie on your back or side. Imagine pulling your tail bone towards your pubic bone, activating the muscles between them, and then pull those muscles upwards as if into the very lower abdominals just above the pubic bone. Sustain this contraction and continue to breathe.

3 Take up a position on hands on knees, so that your hands are directly under your shoulders and your knees are under your hips. Focus on the very lower part of your belly, and scoop it upwards towards your spine. Continue to breathe while sustaining the contraction.

This is a very small muscle contraction, so when activating trans abs, the rest of your body should be relaxed i.e. your shoulders and ribs should not feel awkward, and your back muscles should not be tense.

Stomach scooping is an essential part of all Core Movements.

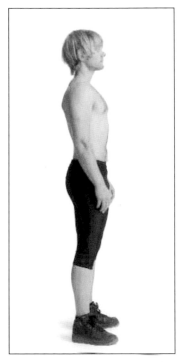

PLAYER WITH RELAXED STOMACH   PLAYER USING 'TRANS ABS'

The movement comes from the stomach, not the ribs or shoulders.

Power Zones

It is helpful to think of your body as having **three power zones.** When using your arms, the forces need to be directed into the upper power zone. This is an imaginary circle at mid-chest level, and includes the stabilising muscles which transmit the arm forces to the midback, as well as the rotator cuff.

If you allow your arm forces to be directed *above* your **upper** power zone, they will be transmitted through longer, thinner muscles to the neck, decreasing the power potential of the arms and increasing the risk of neck pain.

PLAYER ATTEMPTING TO STABILISE HIS SHOULDER
BLADE (SCAPULA) BY ELEVATING IT. FORCES
ARE THEN DIRECTED TO THE NECK

IMPROVED SHOULDER BLADE POSITION.
FORCES DIRECTED INTO MIDBACK

The **central** power zone is the "corset" which encloses your trunk from the bottom of your ribs to the top of your pelvis. It incorporates your abdominal muscles and deep back muscles and acts to stop the forces of your arms and legs being converted into potentially harmful excessive spinal movements. Visualise a strong cylinder around this area and maintain it throughout each exercise.

The **lower** power zone controls the pelvis and thigh, and utilises the gluteal group of muscles. The lower power zone enables you to keep your pelvis level and your knee aligned, which can help to decrease risk of knee and pelvic injury. Visualise a firm ring encircling the pelvis: when using your lower body, imagine containing or pressing your forces between this ring and your feet.

When performing The Core Workout, try to focus on these 'power zones'. If you feel excessive tension in your neck or lower back, relax these areas and concentrate on the muscles in the 'power zones', to provide the support necessary for the exercise that you are performing.

Mental Cues

Above all, it is important to use the correct mental cues for this type of work. The words which go through your mind as you think about an exercise can influence how you perform it, and can change the programming from your brain to your body.

As we have already discussed, words like 'gripping' or 'clenching' the muscles are likely to activate the incorrect muscles. Instead, words like 'lengthening' and 'narrowing' are more helpful. The most important cue, however, is 'effortless control'. If you see a world class sprinter in action you will notice the relaxation around their shoulders and neck, even though they are performing to their maximum ability. A less talented athlete will appear to be using a great deal of effort, which will be evident in excessive tension throughout their body.

Greater effort during a movement does not necessarily facilitate a great performance. Focusing effort into the most effective parts of the body for the job at hand increases efficiency. Visualise yourself performing with the same level of effortlessness that you see in elite athletes by keeping in mind the cue of 'effortless control.

Breathing

It is common to hold your breath when learning the core exercises and this is partly to do with concentration and effort. Try to remind yourself to continue breathing throughout an exercise, and that you are aiming for effortless control.

Pain

Exercises with the ball should make your muscles feel as though they are working, but should not cause pain. If you experience pain during an exercise, consult your doctor

Warm-up and Cool Down

It is advisable that you 'warm-up' prior to starting The Core Workout. Several minutes of light aerobic exercise and progressive stretching (as illustrated in the Flexibility section) will prepare your joints, muscles and cardiovascular system.

When you have finished The Core Workout you are advised to Cool Down by repeating the stretches you performed during the Warm-up. This will reduce the likelihood of muscle soreness and blood pooling.

Warm-up ▶ Stretch ▶ **The Core Workout** ▶ Cool down ▶ Stretch

There are several common errors which will decrease the effectiveness of the movements.

Back Arching

Notice that the hips are raised too high. This is because the back muscles are being used instead of the bottom (glutes or "gluteus maximus"). This usually happens when the "glutes" are either not strong enough, not activating appropriately, or the athlete has a poor movement pattern which has developed over time.

BACK ARCHING   NEUTRAL SPINAL POSITION

Weakness in these bottom muscles is strongly correlated with back injuries. If you are having difficulty achieving a level position, try tipping your pelvis slightly back towards you until you feel your back relax and your bottom tighten.

Shoulder Hitching

The shoulders need to stay low, "away from your ears" to keep the forces from your arms directed into your upper "power zone" at mid-chest level.

SHOULDER HITCHING

NEUTRAL SHOULDER POSITION

Allowing the shoulders to creep up increases stress on the shoulder joints and sends potential harmful forces to the neck.

Chin Poking

Poking of the chin is another compensatory manoeuvre which reinforces poor postural habits and can affect the biomechanics of the neck, shoulders and trunk.

CHIN POKING

CORRECT CHIN POSITION

Knees Deviating Inwards

This error occurs when the muscles of the side and back of the hips (gluteals) fail to control the angle of the thigh (femur).

Concentrate on the muscles that should be performing the movement.

KNEES DEVIATING INWARDS

CORRECT KNEE ALIGNMENT

Hip Flexing

This tends to occur when the abdominals are unable to hold the trunk in neutral. Instead, the relatively strong hip flexors are recruited to prevent the back from sagging, but this error will prevent development of the abdominals as stabilisers.

HIP FLEXING

NEUTRAL HIP ALIGNMENT

Back Sagging

This also occurs when the abdominals do not function adequately to keep the trunk position neutral, but in this case the hip trunk flexors do not compensate.

Stomach Protruding

If you do not perform stomach scooping, you will notice that the middle part of the abdominal wall will protrude, as demonstrated below. This is your rectus abdominis muscle, and it tends to act excessively if your "trans abs" are not activating correctly. This leads to a muscle imbalance and loss of core stability.

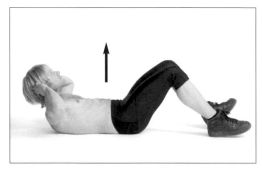

PREDOMINANT RECTUS ADDOMINIS

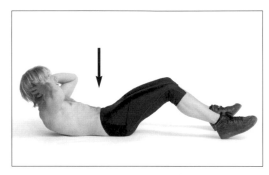

IMPROVED PATTERN USING 'TRANS ABS'

Form is everything

The most important principle is that form is everything. You will not benefit from performing the movements too hard, fast or far for your capabilities. This type of training targets subtle muscles and co-ordination, and if you disregard this principle of form, you will not progress. Worse still, it may allow a risk of injury.

Poor neck Alignment

Back sagging

Hips flexed

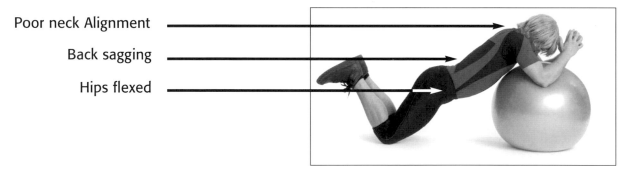

ATHLETE BEYOND HIS CAPABILITIES

This is an example of an athlete who has gone beyond his capabilities, and has lost neutral alignment. As you can see, the back is sagging, the neck is not in neutral alignment, and the hips are flexed. The athlete is gaining no benefit from this exercise, and risks injury.

SAFETY CHECK AND MEDICAL HISTORY

This workout is designed for athletes and fitness enthusiasts, and is not recommended for those who are suffering from acute back or neck injuries, or are just starting a fitness programme. The Swiss exercise ball is highly appropriate to use for all levels of fitness and rehabilitation, but the specific set of exercises outlined in The Core Workout are relatively advanced, and are aimed at high level conditioning.

It is important that you consider you health status prior to following the Core Workout and using the Swiss exercise ball. Exercise involves the risk of injury. If you are in any doubt about your current state of health or how vulnerable you are to injury, seek medical advice before following this programme.

You are strongly advised to complete the following Medical History Questionnaire and if any of your responses are positive please consult your Doctor before following the Core Workout.

MEDICAL HISTORY QUESTIONNAIRE

1. Have you ever suffered from any form of heart complaint?
2. Is there any history of heart disease in your family?
3. Have you ever suffered from epilepsy?
4. Are you recovering from an illness or operation?
5. Have you ever had asthma or suffered from any breathing difficulties?
6. Are you presently taking any form of medication?
7. Are you diabetic?
8. Do you currently have any form of muscle or joint injury?
9. Is there any other reason why it may be inadvisable for you to perform the Core Workout?

Any yes answers?

You should consult your Doctor before performing the exercises outlined in the Core Workout. Check that it is safe for you to go ahead.

PROGRESSION OF EXERCISES

There are many methods for progressing Swiss Ball exercises, but the most significant influences are:

1. The Base Of Support
2. The Plane Of Movement
3. The Length of Lever

Base of Support

The amount of space taken up by the body as it contacts the floor or the wall is the size of the base of support. The base of support can be increased or decreased by widening or narrowing foot or arm contact with the floor or wall. A wider base is more stable and therefore makes an exercise easier. A narrow base provides less stability and is therefore more challenging to control.

Floor bridge using arms to create a wider base by increasing surface contact

Floor bridge with arms across chest which narrows the base by decreasing surface contact

Wall press with feet apart to create a wide base

Wall press with feet together to narrow the base of support.

Wall press on single leg to further narrow the base of support

Seated with feet apart is more stable

Seated with feet together narrows the base of support and is therefore more challenging to control.

Plane of Movement

The direction in which you move your arms will influence the difficulty of the exercise. In exercises such as Floor Bridge, Suspension Bridge and Superman, these arms movement planes will alter the challenge for the trunk stabilisers, especially when a small hand weight is introduced.

The Sagittal Plane

Moving your arms or leg in line with your body is usually the easiest direction to control.

The Coronal Plane

Moving your arms in an upward arc away from your body is easy to control if the movement is done symmetrically (both arms together), but if done with only one arm, this plane is more difficult to control.

Asymmetrical coronal movement

The Transverse Plane

If both arms move symmetrically in an outward arc, the forces on the body are balanced and the movement is easily controlled. However, this is the most challenging plane to control if only one arm is moved.

Asymmetrical transverse movement in Seated position

Symmetrical transverse movement
in Suspension Bridge position

Asymmetrical transverse movement
in Suspension Bridge position

Length of Lever

The length of lever is the distance of the ball from your surface contact point.
The balance and stability challenge on the trunk increases as the ball moves further from the surface contact point.

Changing the lever is a powerful way to increase exercise difficulty: you only need to change the lever by a small amount to increase the trunk demand.

Lengthening the lever by moving the ball further from the contact point

The same principles applies in the "Over The Top" position

In standing the lever is lengthened by moving further from the wall. The stability demand on the body is increased with even a small lever change.

In Suspension Bridge, however, the head must always be correctly supported with the neck in neutral, so lever changes must be done by taking the arms over the head rather than moving the feet away from the ball.

Other progression methods:

Options such as performing exercises with eyes closed, throwing and catching balls, or combining with other equipment such as balance boards or hand weights can also increase the balance and stability challenge of your Swiss Ball exercise.

GETTING STARTED

This is a collection of exercises to teach you to pay attention to how your body moves. Some exercises focus on the upper body primarily and others emphasise the lower body, however in all of the exercises, attention to full body alignment is essential to maximise benefit. Exercise ball work should be viewed as "whole body" exercise.

These are also good movements to practise when beginning rehabilitation after a back injury. Remember to consult your physiotherapist when undertaking exercise after injury.

As with all ball exercises, these movements need to be performed slowly and with good quality. Begin with only four or five repetitions, as you will tire quickly, and this will lead to poor movement. As you become better at the movements, you can start to increase your repetitions. Your target is ten quality repetitions.

A special note: *Athletes often think that these exercises will be too easy, and try to skip over them. Unfortunately, very few of the sportsmen and sportswomen whom we see can perform these exercises well, especially when we slow them down to really see what's going on. No matter how high your athletic ability, it is important that you start to develop an awareness of your body's stabilising systems, and these movements will give you the opportunity to do so.*
Remember: Form is everything!

1. Seated arm raise

This exercise is most effectively performed in front of a mirror.

START POSITION

RAISED ARM POSITION

POOR STABILITY POSITION

Sit with your knees in line with your feet, and your spine in the neutral position. Slowly raise one arm, and watch whether your trunk bends, or the ball moves. If it does, try lengthening your trunk as you lift, and draw your tummy in to control the movement. You should feel an increased tension in the abdomen as your arm approaches its highest point. Now try alternating arms. There should be no sideways trunk movement, no back arching, and no shoulder hitching.

Now try both arms over your head - your spine should stay in its neutral position.

NEUTRAL POSITION

EXTENSION COMPENSATION

FLEXION COMPENSATION

2. Single leg raise

Sit in the neutral position, with your feet together. Scoop your lower abdomen slightly in and "under your tummy button", so that it can assist in stabilising your trunk. Now slowly peel one foot off the floor, bending at the hip joint, not at the waist. Replace the foot, and repeat with the other side.

START POSITION

CORRECT FINISH POSITION

3. Combination lift

If you have mastered 1. and 2., try starting with your arms above your head, and lift one foot from the floor.

Your trunk should stay in its neutral position as you lift the foot. Make sure that you don't shorten one side to make it easier!

CORRECT POSITION
(NEUTRAL SPINE)

POOR POSITION
(FLEXED SPINE)

4. Ab Exploration

This exercise allows you to notice how the abdominal muscles respond to stresses in different directions. Your aim is to keep your back resting comfortably on the floor throughout all movements, and therefore to avoid tipping or arching of the back.

Lie on your back with your knees bent, and the ball in your hands. Gently perform a stomach scoop, and push the ball up towards the ceiling. Now slowly move the ball a small distance over your head: at some point you may feel that your back needs to arch, and at that point you need to narrow at the waist and "scoop" your abdominals a little more to resist that movement.

5. Neutral Bounce

It is important to learn to control the spine while in motion. Many athletes allow their spines to buckle or arch once a dynamic movement is introduced. The seated bounce trains you to recognise and consistently control a neutral spinal position.

Find a neutral spinal position by sitting directly on your seat bones, and stretch both arms up into a streamlined position. By gently squeezing your gluteal (bottom) muscles, start to bounce on the ball, making sure that the spine maintains its neutral curve. As you become more proficient, increase the size of the bounce.

Maintaining a neutral spinal position at all times throughout the bounce action.

Now try moving the ball a little to the left, and a little to the right. Feel the abdominals respond to keep control of your trunk. Then experiment with diagonals, from over the right shoulder across the body to the left hip, and vice versa. If you find that you are better in some directions than others, emphasise the directions which need "topping up".

Ensure that your back has not tightened up, that you are stomach scooping, and that your trunk is resting symmetrically on the floor throughout all movements. The slower you go, the more you notice and the more effective the exercise is for your abdominals.

CREATING A PROGRAMME

If you have performed them well, the above exercises should have taught you to stabilise your trunk as you move your arms and legs. Now it is time to create a core stability programme.

For best results, it is important to structure a core stability programme so that a variety of positions and body parts are emphasised. The next section outlines a collection of exercises which will teach you to activate the major muscle groups involved in core stability. Some of these exercises have progressions - select the most appropriate for your ability level by beginning with the easiest and working towards the level which challenges you. It is important, however, not to progress until an exercise is performed with perfect form, and can be maintained for 10 repetitions. This ensures that you have first developed the co-ordination necessary to perform an exercise correctly, and then achieved the endurance to sustain it. Once you have developed the basic skills trained by these exercises, you can begin to select other exercises to address your needs.

Unlike other workouts, The Core Workout does not designate set numbers of repetitions. This is because there will be individual limitations and differences, and where some exercises may be easy, others will be more challenging. If you try to perform too many repetitions of a challenging exercise, you may lose your form, and no further benefit will be gained once this happens. As a guideline, aim to perform 3-4 sets of between 4 and 10 repetitions.

As previously mentioned, if 10 can be performed well, you have the option to progress the exercise if alternatives are offered, or simply increase the repetitions or sets. The exercises are best performed several times per week, to increase co-ordination and develop form.

To make the most of these exercises, they need to be done with concentration and focus. It is easy to cheat by doing them too fast, and aiming for quantity, not quality. Remember, if it results that you want, there is no easy path. *Form is everything.*

41

KEY ELEMENTS

As a guideline, we have designated a collection of exercises as Key Elements, exercises which provide a foundation around which you can build your programme. These key elements are:

1. the superman
- four point position
- applicable for neck, shoulder, lower back and hip work
- addresses balance of muscles from the upper back down to the hip
- muscular focus on lower trapezius, lower abdominals, gluteals (bottom muscles)

2. wall squat
- upright position
- applicable for lower back, hip, groin, knee and ankle work
- addresses lower power zone and trunk stability
- muscular focus on gluteal muscles, lower abdominals, quadriceps (front of thigh)

3. wall push-up
- upright position
- applicable for neck, shoulder, elbow, mid and lower back work
- addresses upper power zone and trunk stability
- muscular focus on lower abdominals, tricep/pectoral muscles, scapular stabilisers (lower trapezius and serratus anterior)

4. bridge
- supine (face up) position
- applicable for spine from neck to lower back, hip, hamstring and knee work
- addresses lower power zone and trunk stability
- muscular focus on lower abdominals, gluteal muscles, hamstrings

5. over the top
- prone (face down) position
- applicable for neck, shoulder, elbow, mid and lower back
- addresses upper power zone and trunk stability
- muscular focus on shoulder muscles, midback and lower abdominals

This combination targets the major positions, movements and muscle groups and provides a well rounded starter programme. These are Level One exercises, but depending upon your ability, you may need to begin with a level higher. For example, you may find the Wall Squat quite easy, so you may elect to jump to the Level Two version of that exercise, which is the Single Leg Wall Squat. You are still working with a Key Element, but at the level appropriate for you. You can then build around the Key Elements by adding exercises which appeal to you, or which address your needs. Try to select exercises in a variety of positions, as these will work different muscle combinations.

An example Level One programme may be:

Key elements 1-5 ✚ 6. seated leg lift & 7. extended bridge

This combination would target the major positions, movements and muscle groups and provide a well rounded starter programme.

1. The Superman

This exercise is a multipurpose manoeuvre, co-ordinating the whole trunk and teaching sound movement principles. The components can be done alone or in combination.

Level 1 - learning shoulder blade control.
Lie over the ball on all fours. Stabilise the trunk by scooping the stomach up towards the spine and make sure that your head and neck are in a straight line from the shoulders. It is common in this movement to let the head sag down towards the floor, or to tip the head back to try and over use the neck muscles. This will lead to poor movement quality.

START POSITION FOR SUPERMAN

Now try to lift an arm straight in front of you. As your arm lifts, visualise your shoulder blades sliding flat down your rib cage towards your toes. You may find that because of tight muscles you will reach a limit in how far you can lift without your shoulder blades moving up towards your ears. If this is the case, only move as far as you can with good control.
Sustain the position for the count of 5, and then repeat with the other side.

LEVEL 1 - STRAIGHT ARM POSITION WITH SHOULDER BLADE CONTROL

Level 2 - learning pelvic girdle control.
Lie over the ball on all fours. Scoop the stomach up towards the spine to stabilise the trunk as in step one, and slowly straighten one leg out, keeping the toe close to the floor in the initial stages. Use your bottom muscles to create the movement, and to prevent the supporting hip from sagging sideways.

Your finish position should achieve a straight line from ears to toes. The foot should not be above the level of the hip, as this would indicate excessive back muscle activity. You are aiming to keep your hips level and trunk stable, and straighten your hip without causing the lower back to arch.

LEVEL 2 - STRAIGHT LEG POSITION WITH PELVIC GIRDLE CONTROL

Level 3 - putting it together.
Now try combining the two movements with opposite arm and leg

LEVEL 3 - OPPOSITE ARM AND LEG EXTENDED

Level 4 - strong and balanced.
Assume a position over the ball where one leg is extended without overusing the back, and you are not using the arms to balance. Begin with one arm up and the other by your side.

LEVEL 4

Maintaining your trunk position, alternate arms back and forth. After 4-5 repetitions, swap legs. Progress to lifting both arms with one leg extended. After a count of 5, replace the extended leg and extend the other leg.

LEVEL 4 WITH BOTH ARMS EXTENDED

You may also progress to raising up on to your toe.

LEVEL 4 WITH BOTH ARMS EXTENDED AND BALANCING ON YOUR TOE

2. The Wall Squat

This exercise increases hip stability and teaches you to balance the forces across your pelvis. It strengthens the thighs and buttocks. Athletes with poor core stability will tend to overuse their inner thighs and lower back. Stand with the ball at hip level behind your back against the wall. Feet should be shoulder width apart, stomach flattened, bottom squeezing.

Look straight ahead

Keep your shoulders relaxed

Flatten your stomach

Knees in line with hips and ankles

Feet shoulder width apart

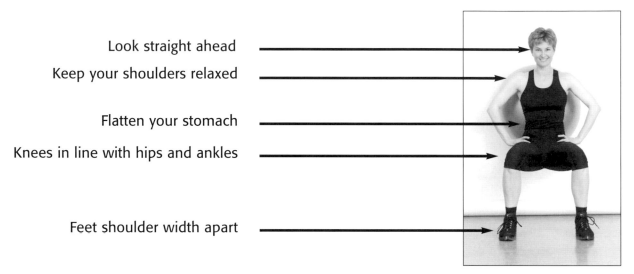

START POSITION FOR WALL SQUAT

1 Slowly roll down the wall, to a point which is no further than 90 degrees at the knee.
2 Hold the position for 10 seconds. Roll back up the ball.

Common errors for the wall squat.
The trunk should remain vertical, with hips and shoulders in line. Two main errors occur:

- Failure to flex the hips
- Sneaking the bottom under the ball

If you can perform a good controlled wall squat, you may progress in a variety of ways.

Progression 1. single heel lift.
Lift one heel and then perform the squat.
This will demand slightly more effort from the other leg.

Progression 2. ski shift.
Squat to a comfortable depth. Keeping shoulders and hips in line move across the ball to one side. Make sure that the hips and shoulders do not lose their alignment.

Progression 3. Cross body lift.
Start in standing with the ball behind you and a small weight positioned at the left hip. As you squat down, lift the weight across your body towards the opposite shoulder. As you move back up, let the weight lower to its start point at the hip. Keep the pelvis level and the hips and knees pointing straight ahead. The hips should not move out to the side as the weight crosses the body!

3. Wall Push-up Level 1

A Wall Push-up can be very challenging if performed correctly, and is recommended as a start point for developing good push-up form. It is particularly useful if recovering from a shoulder injury, beginning to develop upper limb / trunk co-ordination, or learning to maintain a neutral spine position.

The degree of difficulty is dictated by the distance of your feet from the ball.

- Select a distance at which you can control your lumbar spine. As you improve, you may move your feet further from the ball.

- Begin by scooping the stomach and finding your neutral posture. Relax your shoulders and visualise your 'power zone'.

The only joints which will move are your elbows - once you have achieved a neutral spinal position, it will not change throughout the movement.

- As your elbows bend, imagine the force travelling from your elbows into your mid-back. When pushing out, visualise the pushing force coming from the stomach to cue your hips to stay in line with your shoulders.

START POSITION FOR THE WALL PUSH-UP

LEVEL 1 - BENT ELBOW POSITION
FOR THE WALL PUSH-UP

POOR SCAPULA POSITION FOR THE WALL PUSH-UP

Level 1+

To slightly increase the difficulty of the Wall Push up, narrow the base by bringing the feet together

To further increase the difficulty, lengthen the lever by slightly moving your feet further away from the wall.

To increase rotational control, shorten the lever again, and perform the exercise on one leg, making sure that the hips remain parallel to the wall at all times through the motion.

Order of progression

The push-up movement is a very versatile exercise which can be used to target different body parts and functions. You are advised to follow the following progression with the push-up exercises:-

Level 1
Wall Push up

Level 2
Floor Push up

Level 2
Single arm wall push up

Level 3
Full body push up

Push-up Instructions

A note on breathing: It is common during these higher levels of the push-up for athletes to hold their breath. This is not safe or effective practice. Instead, it is advisable to breathe in as you bend your elbows, and breathe out when pushing up. This helps to maintain your breathing cycle and facilitate an abdominal contraction, which is essential for correct performance of the push-up.

Level 2 - Single Arm Push-up

This is a challenging exercise for athletes of any level. Assume a starting position as for the Wall Push-up. Release one hand, and support the arm to be exercised by lowering the shoulder blade and flattening it into the rib cage.

The movement principles are the same as for the Wall Push-up, however now you must concentrate on keeping the planes of your shoulders and hips parallel with the wall.

SINGLE ARM WALL PUSH-UP

POOR SCAPULA AND TRUNK POSITION THE
SINGLE ARM WALL PUSH-UP

Level 2 - The Floor Push-up

This exercise coordinates the trunk with the shoulder girdle. It strengthens chest triceps and abdominal muscles.

Place the ball against the wall, and kneel in front of it with your hands comfortably apart.

START POSITION FOR THE PUSH-UP

Keep shoulders down and shoulder blades flat on the ribs

Pull your abs in for a neutral back

Resist the urge to poke chin

FINISH POSITION FOR THE PUSH-UP

Level 2+

The Floor Press can be made more difficult by moving the ball away from the wall.

Progress to a **Level 3 - Full Body Push-up.** Perform the exercise above in full push-up position. This will demand a great deal of abdominal control. Make sure that you can achieve a controlled movement with the ball against the wall before trying the exercise without wall support.

FULL BODY PUSH-UP START POSITION

Scoop the abdominals up towards the spine and keep your shoulders away from your ears to maintain alignment..

FULL BODY PUSH-UP

LEVEL 4 - FULL BODY PUSH-UP WITH FEET ELEVATED

4. The Bridge

This exercise trains buttock and hamstring strength as well as trunk stability. If you want to focus on your 'glutes', perform the exercise with the ball close to your hips. If you wish to focus more on hamstrings, start with the ball slightly further out.

Lie on your back with your feet on the ball. Initially, use your elbows for support if necessary. Scoop your stomach up and in and check that your neck is relaxed.

START POSITION PRIOR TO THE BRIDGE

Tighten your 'glutes' and slowly peel your hips from the floor by pressing down on the ball.

It is important to visualise pushing down through your feet, to help to focus your effort into your legs rather than your back. Aim to keep your back relatively relaxed while working hard on your buttocks and legs. To do this, you may need to tip your pelvis back slightly towards you which will help to counteract a common tendency towards back arching.

LEVEL 1 - EXTENDED HIPS POSITION
FOR THE BRIDGE

LEVEL 2 - BRIDGE WITH ARMS ABOVE

LEVEL 2 - BRIDGE WITH ARM TO THE SIDE

Once you can balance in this position:

- progress to placing your arms across your chest, which will decrease your base of support.

- To progress further, start with both arms up to the ceiling and then move one arm out to the side. Bring it back to the centre and repeat with the other side.

- To further progress, lift one leg off the ball.

LEVEL 3 - SINGLE LEG BRIDGE

Another option is to perform the Bridge with straight legs, and progress with arm movements in the same manner as above.

LEVEL 1 - STRAIGHT LEG BRIDGE

Progress to lifting one leg off the ball as in the bent leg Bridge.

LEVEL 3 - STRAIGHT SINGLE LEG BRIDGE

5. Over the Top

This exercise builds abdominal strength and teaches good alignment. Begin by kneeling behind the ball.

Push out over the ball and support yourself with your hands. The ball should be positioned at mid thigh level. Check neck alignment, and make sure your shoulders haven't crept up towards your ears. Try to pull your stomach up to your spine so that the lower back and hips are straight. If you cannot keep this position, roll slightly back onto the ball to decrease the

START POSITION FOR OVER THE TOP

leverage. Check your *lower back alignment* - common errors are either to sag, or to pull with your hip muscles. Instead, imagine a straight line from your ears to your ankles.

LEVEL 1 - CORRECT OVER THE TOP POSITION

INCORRECT OVER THE TOP POSITION

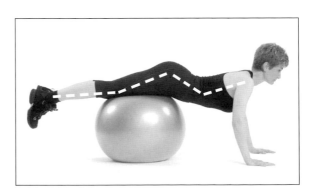

INCORRECT OVER THE TOP POSITION

Once you have established the basic position, push with your arms so that the body moves back towards the ball, keeping a straight body line. Then pull with the arms so that the body moves forward over the ball, keeping a straight body line. Your trunk should not sag or bend in the middle – try to maintain a long, straight shape throughout the movement. Once you can keep the correct balance, use the shoulders and arms to move the body over the ball in a circle. The trunk should stay still, supported by the abdominals, while the shoulders produce the movement. Once again, maintain a strong , straight body line, with no hip or spine movement.

LEVEL 2 - PUSHING BACKWARDS AND PULLING FORWARDS

Do not produce the movement from the spine. Repeat to the right.

VIEW FROM ABOVE WHEN CIRCLING LEFT

Note that the movement is generated from the arms, and that the trunk does not bend to create the movement. To progress, start with the ball further towards your feet - the further it is from your trunk, the greater the demand on your abdominals. Remember, even if the ball needs to be at the upper thigh level in order for you to achieve good form, you are still gaining benefit.

The following exercises can be used to develop your programme. Try to achieve variety in positions and action as well as working upper and lower body muscle groups.

1 | The Walkout

This exercise takes your body through an arc which works your abdominals to stabilise and control. Sit comfortably on the ball with neck and shoulders in neutral.

STARTING POSITION FOR THE WALKOUT

Tuck your chin in and start to walk slowly down and away from the ball, keeping stomach **scooped in.**

MID-WAY POSITION FOR THE WALKOUT

Try to keep the **chin in** and the **stomach scooped** until you reach a point where your shoulders are resting on the ball. Relax your back and support yourself using your buttocks. This is called the ***extended bridge position.***

Neutral head position   Neutral back position   Stomach scooped

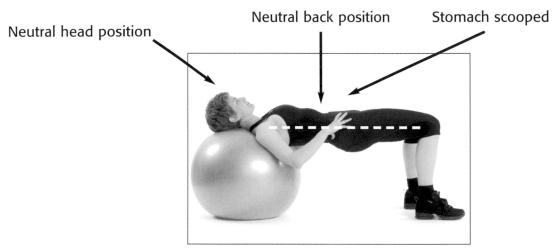

EXTENDED BRIDGE POSITION

Begin to walk back up the ball, curling from the chin and keeping the stomach flat.

WALKING UP THE BALL

2 | The Suspension Bridge

This exercise trains your gluteal muscles to work with your abdominals to control your trunk and pelvis. Begin with a walkout, and stay in a position where your shoulders are resting on the ball, and your stomach 'scooped' in.

Check your neck alignment, and that your back is not arching.

LEVEL 1 - SUSPENSION BRIDGE POSITION

Level 1

● Reach your arms up towards the ceiling and slowly move one arm out to the side. Try not to let your body rotate. Slowly bring the arm back to the start position and repeat with the other arm (not illustrated).

If you can perform this movement well, you may progress to **Level 2**. Keeping your pelvis level and your buttocks squeezing, lift the toes of one foot and the heel of the other. Now swap sides, so that the trunk is in the same position, but the heel/toe lift is opposite. Alternate back and forth for a count of six, then rest. This equals one set. Aim eventually for ten sets.

Remember to keep your pelvis level -- we often see the hips sinking slowly towards the floor, and this means that your buttocks have switched off!

To rest between sets, you have two options. If you feel quite confident, you can walk back up the ball, as in The Walkout, or if not, you can simply drop your hips.

Level 3

Start with your feet closer together.
Focus your mind into whichever buttock is going to support you and slowly peel the other heel off the floor. Scoop the abdominals, and straighten the knee so that you are only supported on one leg. Count to 5, replace the leg and repeat on the other side.

To avoid cheating by arching your back, keep your focus on your supporting buttock as you perform this exercise.

LEVEL 3 - SUSPENSION BRIDGE POSITION

Focus hard on your supporting buttock before you lift your leg. You'll want to cheat by arching your back - try to refocus on your buttock. Replace the leg, and repeat on the other side.

Progress to lifting the leg and straightening the knee, holding for 10 seconds. If this is easy for you, try moving one arm to the side and back while sustaining a neutral position on one leg.

LEVEL 3 - EXTENDED LEG POSITION WITH ARM VARIATIONS

Remember: there is no advantage to performing a more advanced progression if you are unable to maintain neutral in the previous movement.

You now have the option of increasing the demands of the exercise by moving your arms or introducing a weight.

LEVEL 4 - EXTENDED LEG POSITION
WITH A WEIGHT

3 | The Sway

This exercise trains trunk alignment and hip stability. Walk out into the extended bridge position, and let your arms fall out to the side. Check that your neck and lower back are neutral (it is easy to slip into back arching) and that your abdominals and buttocks are working.

START POSITION FOR THE SWAY

Keep your trunk & hips in line and without moving your feet, shift over the ball to the left. The ball will roll under your shoulders, towards your right. Feel your weight transfer to your left buttock.

LEVEL 2 - SWAY TO THE LEFT

LEVEL 2 - SWAY TO THE RIGHT

Your legs should remain pointing forward. If you find your knees moving in the opposite direction to your shoulders, you have released your abdominals! Repeat on the other side.

63

4 | The Ham Sandwich

Begin in the extended bridge position. Keeping your hips level, push with your feet so that your knees straighten slightly.

LEVEL 1 - PUSH OUT FOR
THE HAM SANDWICH

FINISH POSITION FOR
THE HAM SANDWICH

Keeping your hips from sagging towards the floor, pull with your feet until your knees are bent. **Repeat up to 10 repetitions.**

NOTE: This will seem very easy if you do not concentrate on keeping your hips absolutely level. The focus will be on your abdominals, buttocks, and hamstrings contracting, and the muscles on the tops of your thighs and hips stretching.

When you have mastered the Ham Sandwich, progress to a single leg Ham Sandwich. This will combine the skill of the advanced Suspension Bridge with extra hamstring effort.

Assume the same start position as for the two leg exercise, then raise one leg to achieve the advanced Suspension Bridge. Concentrate on keeping your pelvis level. Now pull yourself forward towards your feet as in the double leg Ham Sandwich.

LEVEL 3 - SINGLE LEG HAM SANDWICH

5 | The Hamstring Pull

This exercise trains buttock strength and provides an intense hamstring workout. Lie on your back with your feet on the ball. Scoop your stomach, and check neck alignment.

Level 1

Squeezing your glutes keeps the hips straight

Keep your back relaxed - if you cannot do this, try tipping your pelvis slightly back towards you

START POSITION PRIOR TO HAMSTRING PULL

LEVEL 2 - EXTENDED HIPS POSITION FOR THE HAMSTRING PULL

Remember to support this position by squeezing the buttocks, not by arching the back.

Level 2

Once you can balance in this position, let your feet push the ball out a small distance. You must only push the ball as far as you can without letting your back arch, and no further.

Maintain a neutral spine - if you push out too far, you will arch your back and over use your back muscles. Check the alignment of your neck and lower back. Now pull the ball back towards you until you are back to the start

LEVEL 2 - FINISH POSITION FOR THE HAMSTRING PULL

position. Repeat the movement at a controlled speed. To make this exercise slightly more difficult, lift your arms up towards the ceiling while performing the movement.

10 | The Windmill

This is a level 2 exercise

This exercise teaches the gluteal muscles to support the back by controlling your hip angle, and trains the abdominals to both stabilise against and create rotational movement.

Begin by lying over the ball on your stomach, with your feet on the floor. Scoop your abdominals up towards your spine. In order to level your body, squeeze your gluteal muscles to straighten the hip. Your initial attempt will probably involve trying to use the back muscles to pull your shoulders up; try to relax the back and focus on pulling from the gluteals.

LEVEL 2 - START POSITION FOR THE WINDMILL

Notice that the athlete's back is not straining to lift the shoulders, but is instead maintaining a fairly neutral position. Preventing over-activity in the lower back muscles is the most difficult part of this exercise.

Now that you have achieved a reasonable position, turn your upper trunk so that one hand touches the floor. Pull yourself back into the start position by using the abdominals. Now tilt in the other direction.

WINDMILL TURN TO THE LEFT

WINDMILL TURN TO THE RIGHT

Level 3 You may also progress by putting your feet against the wall. They will need to be positioned below the level of the hip to maintain a stable position.

As during the floor based Windmill, turn your upper trunk so that one hand touches the floor.

LEVEL 3 - START POSITION FOR THE WALL WINDMILL

WINDMILL POSITION TO THE LEFT

Now return to the start position and rotate to the other side.

WINDMILL POSITION TO THE RIGHT

71

11 | The Body Spin

This is a level 3 exercise

This exercise requires multiple actions of the abdominal muscles. They must control the back angle, but also initiate and control rotational movement.

Begin by lying over the ball on your lower ribs, with your feet on the floor. Scoop your abdominals up towards your spine. In order to level your body, squeeze your gluteal muscles to straighten the hip.

Your arms are out in front of you and your spine should be neutral.

Squeeze glutes   Flat back

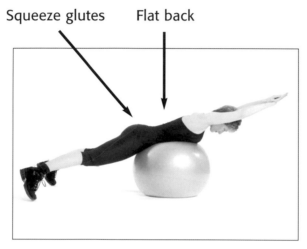

START POSITION FOR THE BODY SPIN

Very slowly begin to turn your upper body to one side, allowing your feet to face the direction in which you are moving. Try not to let your body bend at the waist.

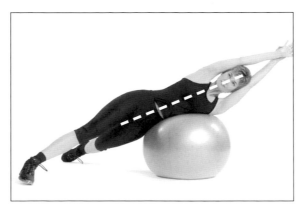

FINISH POSITION FOR THE BODY SPIN

- Straighten your arms
- Do not bend at the waist

Slowly turn back to the starting position, feeling the focus in your abdominals as they control your speed. Repeat to the other side.

FINISH POSITION FOR THE BODY SPIN (OPPOSITE DIRECTION)

If you find it difficult to secure your feet on the floor, use a wall as a safeguard.

Maintaining alignment, pull the ball back towards you a short distance, then push it away a short distance. The movement should only occur at the shoulders, not the back.

Progress to a full body Ab Burner. Gradually straighten your body, so that there is a straight line from the back of your head to your knees.

Push down strongly into ball

LEVEL 3 - LONG LEVER AB BURNER

LEVEL 3 - LONG LEVER AB BURNER
MOVE ELBOWS FORWARD TO FINISH POSITION

Now move the ball away a short distance with your arms. If your back wants to sag, do not go any further. **Pull in hard with the abdominals** towards the spine to maintain alignment, and move the ball back towards you.

Do not push beyond your limits - if you cannot maintain a neutral lower back by scooping your abdominals, you have gone too far. This will not make you stronger or more stable.

14 | The Mogul Squat

THE MOGUL SQUAT

You can introduce a sports specific element to lower limb control by progressing to the Mogul Squat (advanced). Begin with the single leg wall squat. With a quick push through your feet, change the angle of your lower legs by lifting and shifting your heels outwards. As you bring your weight back down onto the whole feet, let your knees absorb the movement by bending slightly. Try to maintain this control through the knees, rather than letting your hips sag sideways.

Caution: Do not try to keep the feet planted and rotate through the knees - this will cause harmful stress through the knee joint. Most of the foot should lift from the floor when shifting position.

Notice that the ball will rotate as your hips turn slightly to follow your leg. To ensure good form, imagine a line going across the front of your pelvis, parallel to the floor. Keep this line parallel throughout the movement. Loss of neutral would reflect in that line dipping towards the floor on one side.

If you have mastered the double mogul squat, and you can perform a good normal single leg squat, you can progress to a single leg mogul squat. Remember not to plant your foot and twist through your knee: you must push and lift the foot slightly to be able to turn safely.

15 | The Squat Ball Thrust

Begin in the Over the Top position. Concentrating on your abdominals, pull the ball towards your body. Maintaining a neutral position for your shoulder blades, head and lower back, move the ball back out to the start position. Visualise a long straight line from your ears to your toes, and your abdominals pulled up to make your waist narrow.

START POSITION FOR SQUAT BALL THRUST

Control this position by keeping your abdominals pulled in and squeezing your glutes. Do not allow your shoulders to hitch towards your ears and do not hold your breath. Slowly extend your legs while keeping your back flat and hips up.

SQUAT BALL THRUST FINISH POSITION

Return to the start position for repeat slowly and controlled. To progress, try this with a single leg.

16 | The Caterpillar

This is a level 3 exercise

This exercise incorporates a second ball to introduce two sources of instability. Assume a position where your hands are on one ball and knees on another. Scoop abdominals and try to attain a neutral position for head, shoulders and lower back.

THE CATERPILLAR

Now try and move the ball from side to side with your knees. Progress to moving the arms and legs in opposite directions. Now try pushing the front ball slightly forward and bring it back then try pushing the back ball away, and bring it back.

You may combine any of these directions, and add ideas of your own, such as arms moving clockwise and knees anti-clockwise.

17 | The Pendulum Roll

This is a level 2 exercise

Begin in an extended bridge position with your arms towards the ceiling. Slowly roll your shoulders and arms to one side, allowing the ball to roll slightly in the opposite direction. Concentrate on keeping your pelvis level and as your arms move. You will need to keep focused on the 'glutes' pushing up firmly on the side towards which your arms are moving. Using control from the abdominals, slowly rotate in the other direction.

START POSITION FOR
THE PENDULUM ROLL

PENDULUM ROLL TO THE RIGHT

PENDULUM ROLL TO THE LEFT

You may progress to using a weight to increase the demands of the Pendulum Roll. Remember however, that even a very light weight can greatly increase the intensity of this exercise.

PENDULUM ROLL WITH A WEIGHT
(START POSITION)

PENDULUM RIGHT WITH WEIGHT

SKILL BUILDERS

Skill builders are exercises that introduce a more dynamic component to your core stability work. Most of the preceding Core Exercises aim to develop primary muscle strength and co-ordination, training trunk stability by using forces exerted by your arms and legs under relatively controlled conditions.

Now that you have a grounding in Core Stability, you can introduce exercises which demand faster reactions, using balance, momentum and ballistic principles to encourage your body to react appropriately to less predictable forces.

1 | 4-3-2 Point Balance

Stand behind the ball with knees in contact with the ball and hands resting on it. Rock forward gently until your feet lift from the ground and gradually tighten your buttocks. When you are balanced, rock slightly from side to side, forward and back or in small circles, maintaining your neutral posture.

- Do not hunch your shoulders

- Scoop your abs in and squeeze your glutes

Focus on avoiding the Common Errors and maintain your posture when moving on the Fitball. When this is easy, raise one hand, so that you are now balancing on three points instead of four.

Once again, attempt to move the ball slightly.

If you are able to progress, try replacing your arm and extended one leg.

- Do not arch your back

- Tuck your chin in

Place particular emphasis on squeezing the buttock of the leg you have extended. Once you are comfortable with 3 point balance, 2 point balance can be attempted by lifting opposite arm and leg. However, this is a very unstable position, and should be approached with caution and care to prevent falling. If your balance is not secure, or if you are at risk should you fall e.g. you have decreased bone density, or joint instability, do not choose this exercise. 2 point balance is actually more difficult than kneeling on the ball.

4 POINT BALANCE

3 POINT BALANCE (ONE ARM)

3 POINT BALANCE (ONE LEG)

2 POINT BALANCE (ONE ARM & ONE LEG)

2 | Titanic

This exercise is a level two + exercise. It can be practised if you have mastered an advanced superman. Its purpose is to strengthen and coordinate the hip extensor and back extensor muscle groups.

Place the ball under your hips, and your feet on the wall near the floor. Allow your body to rest over the ball, so that the hips are slightly bent. Scoop abdominals. Keeping fingertips on the floor, squeeze the hips forward into the ball, using the glutes strongly. If you feel secure, you can withdraw the fingertips, so that you are holding on mainly with your glutes. Do not raise the trunk above the level of the hips, as this will use excessive back extensor muscle activity. Count to 5.

3 | Balance Challenge

Stand behind ball with knees in contact and hands resting on the ball. Rock forwards until your feet are off the ground, and gradually tighten your buttocks. Shift the weight off your hands, and try to kneel on the ball without hanging on.

Avoid using your feet to 'cup' the ball and bring your hips forward by squeezing your glutes.

If this is easy, try to clap your hands in front and then behind you or above your head and behind your waist. Count your claps or time duration on the ball.

Bring your hips forward

Squeeze your glutes

BALANCE CHALLENGE

83

4 | The Wrestle

This exercise is excellent for developing rotational trunk control, dynamic balance and abdominal strength.

Kneel on the ball facing each other. Join hands, or link forearms so that you have a strong hold on each other. Your task now is to exert enough pressure on your partner to challenge his or her balance, but it is also your responsibility to prevent them from losing their balance completely.

THE WRESTLE

In order to do this you must think about the upper power zones, so that your shoulders are relaxed and the forces on your arms are directed to mid chest level, and also the lower power zones, so that y our glutes stabilise your hips, and your abdominals keep your spine in neutral.

Increase the difficulty greater rotational force via an 'arm wrestle.'

THE ARM WRESTLE

5 | Slap Hands

This version of the kneeling balance exercise requires faster balance reactions and good reflexes.

Kneel on the ball facing each other. Begin finger tip to finger tip, and then one of you will attempt to quickly slap the other's hand, while he or she tries to avoid being caught. Maintain your neutral alignment as you concentrate on your hands!

SLAP HANDS ON THE BALL

6 | Sport Specific Skills

The sport specific drills incorporate hand and eye coordination with balancing on the ball. The following examples relate to the sports of netball and rugby.

Balanced Shoulder Pass

Follow the same guidelines as for the Balance Challenge and adhere to the correct passing and catching technique for netball.

BALANCED SHOULDER PASS

Balanced Lateral Pass
You may apply the same principles for other sports

BALANCED LATERAL PASS

7 | Balistic Push-ups

These exercises increase the demand on your shoulder and scapular stabilisers, as well as requiring good abdominal holding ability to keep the spine in neutral. They should only be performed after you have mastered the standard pushups detailed in the Core Exercises.

1. Keep it up!

This exercise introduces a ballistic element to upper body training. Set the ball at shoulder height in a corner. Following the principles for the Wall Push-up (neutral posture with a flat stomach) with particular emphasis on keeping your shoulder blades low and flat, perform a single arm wall push-up, and quickly swap hands so that you catch the ball before it falls. Make sure that you generate the outward push from the arm and not by shifting your body weight back from the hips. Your trunk should remain neutral throughout the exercise.

DYNAMIC SINGLE ARM WALL PUSH-UP

Begin with slow push-ups and a quick change, and gradually increase the speed of your hand changeover. Remember, keep your shoulders and hips parallel to the wall and do not let your back sag. Progress to positioning the ball against a flat wall.

DYNAMIC SINGLE ARM WALL PUSH-UP AGAINST A FLAT WALL

2. Plyo Push-up

Place the ball in a corner, and kneel a comfortable distance from it. Before trying this ballistic push-up, perform a normal kneeling pushup as featured on page 49, so that you know that you can control your lumbar spine with your abdominals from that distance.

Keeping your body straight, tip forward to catch yourself by landing on the ball with both hands, and push yourself up again.

DOUBLE HAND PLYO PUSH-UP

The force should be absorbed through your elbows, and into your "upper power zone" at mid chest level, not by letting your shoulders hunch up towards your ears! Repeat. When you have mastered the double hand pushup on your knees, progress to the alternate hand pushup. This increases the demand on your shoulder stabilisers, and requires a great deal of trunk stability to maintain a neutral lumbar spine.

ALTERNATE HAND PLYO PUSH-UP

The alternate hand push-up can also be done with the ball against
a flat wall to reduce the stability of the ball.

8 | Walk the Walk

The movement is similar to the Squat Ball Thrust except you pull the ball with one leg at a time and walk with your hands. Without your feet touching the ground, attempt to cover a distance while balancing on the ball.

WALK THE WALK START POSITION

Once your legs have flexed to a controlled position, walk with your hands until you reach the start position.

WALK THE WALK LEG MOVEMENT

WALK THE WALK LEG MOVEMENT

9 | The Handspring

This exercise trains dynamic trunk stability, and adds a ballistic component to further challenge the shoulders.

Start in a squat behind the ball. Activate your abdominals by bringing them up and in, as these will be needed to maintain a neutral spine throughout the movement.

HANDSPRING START POSITION

Pushing through the legs, "spring" over the ball until you can catch your body weight with your hands. You are aiming to prevent your lower back from dipping towards the floor, and to keep your shoulder blades flat on your rib cage.

  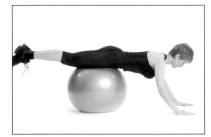

The most common errors are shoulder blades hunching up towards the ears, and the lower back dropping towards the floor. Try to keep your trunk neutral, and absorb the force through your elbows.

When you can perform this exercise well, increase the force with which you push through your legs. This will increase your speed over the ball, and requires a higher level of control from your upper body to control the momentum.

When you are confident performing this exercise, you can progress to springing forward onto one hand. Remember to begin slowly again - landing on one hand is significantly more difficult than landing on two!

HANDSPRING (ONE ARM LANDING POSITION)

10 | The Twisting Spring

Using the same principles as for the Handspring, we are going to introduce an increased demand on the whole body by adding lower body movement.

Begin in a squat behind the ball as for the Handspring. This time, after your hands contact the floor, bring both knees up to the side for the last part of the movement. As you move back, push out from the legs and turn your body so that you land straight with both legs together.

THE TWISTING SPRING

Repeat to the other side. Once this becomes easy, you can try landing on your right hand as you bring your knees up to the left side, and vice versa!

11 | The Sprinter

This exercise was devised when working with sprinters to increase the strength and efficiency of their hip flexion. It is aimed at building a stable anchor for the muscles to pull from, and to decrease ineffective movement patterns.

Stand with the ball between you and the wall, and your feet together as you would for the Wall Squat. Activate your abdominals by bringing the stomach up and in, and tighten the 'glutes' of your supporting side.

THE SPRINTER

Keeping the pelvis level and 'open', i.e. facing straight ahead, and your lower back neutral, slowly raise the other knee to a height which you feel that you can control. Control means that you do not let the knee deviate inwards and that you do not 'hip hitch,' which avoids using the hip flexor muscles by trying to substitute the muscles on the side of your trunk.

During the movement, your bottom should not sneak under the ball, and your supporting side should not sag. You are aiming for a straight pattern of leg action with minimal trunk or ball movement.

When you have mastered this exercise at a slow speed, begin to introduce the sprinting arm movement and increase your speed of leg movement. Do not be tempted to bend forward. Keep thinking of being tall and light, and isolating your effort to your lower power zone.

GOOD FORM

POOR FORM

POOR FORM

This is a difficult exercise to perform well, and requires a high level of co-ordination. The illustrations above show deviations from neutral whereby the athlete is rotating inwards with the right leg and hip hitching.   If you are having difficulty performing this movement with the ball, practise with your back directly against a wall, which will provide greater support. **Remember your form!**

12 | The Pullover

This is a very high level exercise, and it requires good coordination, balance and gluteal/ abdominal strength. It trains the trunk to remain stable against the resistance of both arms and legs.

START POSITION FOR THE PULLOVER

Assume a suspension bridge position. Lift one foot from the floor and straighten the knee, as for the higher level suspension bridge. Extend both arms straight over the head to point at the wall.

Make sure that your pelvis is level, that your stomach is pulled up and in, and that your "glutes" are working hard. Bring both arms over the head with the elbows bent, at the same time as bending your hip and knee towards you.

THE PULLOVER

After 4-5 repetitions, swap legs.

You will be strongly tempted to let your hips bend so that your bottom sinks towards the floor. Your objective is to maintain a neutral spine, and this will require a great deal of focus on your supporting buttock.

INCORRECT PULLOVER

13 | The Kickout

This is also a very high level exercise, which requires a great deal of trunk stability, abdominal strength, coordination and balance.

Stage One:
Prop the ball against a wall, and assume an Ab Burner start position, with your weight directed down through your elbows. Push firmly down into the ball to prevent your shoulders from hunching. You abdominals should be pulled up towards your spine, and your back in neutral.

THE KICKOUT START POSITION

Without letting this spine position alter, bring one knee up to ninety degrees. Maintaining the spinal position, extend your leg back out to the start position. Repeat 4-5 times.

THE KICKOUT WITH WALL SUPPORT

As you improve, you may begin to increase your speed of movement, and if your very confident, progress to Stage Two and move the ball away from the wall.

Stage 3++

Assume a Full Ab Burner position with the ball away from the wall. You are going to perform the same leg movement as for the previous exercise, however this time as your knee moves towards your stomach, you will move the ball in slightly with your elbows.

THE KICKOUT FROM A FULL AB BURNER POSITION

As your leg extends back out, you will move the ball forward with your elbows. Try to limit the amount of outward movement of the ball to a range which you can control, as illustrated below.

Loss of neutral will often result in back rounding and chin poking.

OUTWARD POSITIONING DURING THE KICKOUT

INCORRECT KICKOUT POSITION

DOUBLE TROUBLE

It can be challenging and fun to work with a partner and/or two balls, and incorporate other factors, such as unpredictability and reaction speed, to further advance your stabilising skills.

A few guidelines which must be borne in mind regarding partner and two ball exercises to maximise their benefit, and maintain safety.

Communication

When beginning partner exercises, you will need to let each other know when you are going to move or push, particularly when assuming the start position. Some exercises, e.g. the double squat, will need an agreement as to when you will both put full weight against the ball and each other, prior to beginning the movement.

Pacing

When beginning partner exercises, you will need to make direction changes slow and gradual, until you and your partner learn to react with the correct muscles. If you begin with rapid direction changes, and are not adequately prepared or trained, you will tend to activate incorrect muscles, decreasing the effectiveness of the exercise, and increasing the risk of injury. Ideally, you will master unpredictable changes of direction at a slow speed, and gradually increase with practice.

Form

Partner exercises can introduce an element of competition, which can be a positive influence, but is of no use if you sacrifice form for it. Remember that you are working as a two person team aiming for optimal results, and that those results are dependent entirely on the quality of your performance. All the same form tips apply - stomach flattening, neutral alignment, head position, power zones.

1 Standing Double Press

Face each other with the ball at mid-chest height between you. Slowly press into the ball, until your weight is supported by your arms.

Perform a push-up against the ball, remembering to maintain neutral alignment from your head through to your lower back. As one partner performs the push-up, the other stabilises. If you're game you may both attempt to perform a push-up at the same time!

STANDING DOUBLE PRESS START POSITION

2 Standing Single Arm Press

Face each other with the ball at mid-chest height between you.

Slowly press into the ball, until your weight is supported by your arm. Remember to keep your shoulder blade flat against your rib cage, and the force directed into your upper power zone. Perform a push-up against the ball, remembering to maintain neutral alignment from your head through to your lower back.

STANDING SINGLE ARM PRESS START POSITION

3 | Moving Press

This can be done with two hands or one, depending on the level of difficulty required.
Face each other with one hand each holding the ball at mid-chest height between you.
Slowly press into the ball, until your weight is partially supported by your arm.
Designate who will lead the movement first.

Slowly begin to move the ball through a variety of angles, diagonally, up, down, side to side. You may eventually reach a stage where there is no designated leader, and the movement becomes a smooth and fluid exchange between the two of you. This level of fast automatic reaction without effort is an excellent result!

To progress, increase speed, or increase the force exerted through the ball. Do not be tempted to abandon good neutral alignment - this will decrease your power and control.

To further progress your balance, try using two hands and one foot.

4 | Double Pump

Face your training partner with two balls held between you at chest height. Each bend your knees slightly to take up a stable position. Make sure that your abdominal and gluteal muscles are working to keep your back and pelvis neutral. Keeping your shoulders down and your necks "long", each push forward with your right hand, while letting your left be pushed back. Alternate this movement keeping good form throughout your body.

DOUBLE PUMP ACTION

Once you have achieved a good feel for this movement, gradually increase your pressure on the balls until your arms are working to partially resist the push from your partner. The balls should still move through a full range of motion, but you will need to increase your focus on your power zones to control the forces on your trunk. You will probably ave to use more "abs" and "glutes", and remind yourself to keep your shoulders down.

When you have achieved good form, you may try to increase your speed.

5 | Prone Push-up

Assume a push-up position on opposite sides of the ball. Remember the alignment cues which you have learned from the individual push-up - the same rules apply!

Alternate the pushup i.e. one holds while the other moves. DO NOT FORGET YOUR FORM!

PRONE PUSH-UP

6 | Double Ramp

As in the single ramp (p64) this exercise can be done on knees or feet, depending on your ability

Hold this position as both players try to move the ball in small degrees in any direction. The challenge is to resist the other player's movement choice.

DOUBLE RAMP

Do not hold this exercise for too long - this level of stabilising is quite advanced. Thirty seconds is a good starting time.

7 | Double Arm Stabiliser

Refer back to the Arm Stabiliser (p58). Assume a position on opposite sides of the ball as pictured.

Each player tries to move the ball a small amount in any direction against the resistance of the other. Do not exceed thirty seconds to begin with.

DOUBLE ARM STABILISER START POSITION

8 | Double Dip

Assume a starting position as for the Double Arm Stabiliser and perform alternating dips i.e. one holds while the other dips.

DOUBLE DIP

9 | Double Hip Lift

Lie on your backs with your feet on the ball. Lift the hips by pressing down into the ball with your feet. Remember the form tips from the hamstring pull - stomach scooped, gluteals squeezing, and no back arching. Now try and vary the position of the ball against each other, but try and keep your pelvis level.

DOUBLE HIP LIFT

10 | Single leg Hip Lift

The aim is the same i.e. to move the ball in different directions against each other's resistance.

SINGLE LEG HIP LIFT

11 | Trunk Controller

Lie on your backs with your feet on the ball. Scoop stomachs, and increase the pressure on the ball slightly to raise it off the floor.

DOUBLE LEG TRUNK CONTROLLER

Move the ball against each other in any combination of directions. The aim is to keep the trans abs working (no stomach protruding) and the trunk flat on the floor. If this is too easy, progress to the Single Leg Trunk Controller.

12 | Single Leg Trunk Controller

The same principles apply as above, but this time try controlling the ball with one leg. **(HINT: you'll need your gluteals to control your hip and leg).**

You will need to concentrate on your abdominals to keep your stomach flat and your pelvis flat and level.

SINGLE LEG TRUNK CONTROLLER

Now try it with your opposite feet together. Both legs move independently.

SINGLE LEG WITH FEET TOGETHER

13 | Double Leg Squat

The trickiest part of this exercise is balancing your body weights. To do this, you both need to be able to push your backs into the ball, at the same time. This can be done even when you have very different body weights, by communicating at the time when you need to push against the other person. This is best done slowly. Your feet will need to start away from the ball, so that you can achieve an end position where your knee is no further out than your ankle.

Once you have achieved a balanced starting position, proceed to perform a squat, remembering to use the gluteals to control the movement and the position of the thigh.

DOUBLE LEG SQUAT

14 | Single Leg Squat

Try the same exercise, this time with one person bracing while the other performs a single leg squat.. If you're a really talented team, try both with one leg

Correct posture   Poor posture

SINGLE LEG SQUAT (ADVANCED)

SINGLE LEG SQUAT (ADVANCED)

105

15 | The Stacks

These exercises are called "stacks" because they involve the ability to withstand an external force, stacked on the ability to control rotation, stacked on the ability to maintain a stable neutral position. They involve two people, and one or two balls. Stacks can be performed in any position relevant to the sport.

Starter stack
Stand with feet apart and two foot lengths from the wall, as in the wall squat. Bend the knees slightly, pull the abdominals in and activate the gluteal muscles to provide a strong lower power zone. Hold the ball at mid chest level, and set your shoulder blades so that they are low and flat on your rib cage.

Your partner will now exert gentle pressure against the ball in different directions.

STARTER STACK

The Sway stack
Follow the principles for The Sway (Core Exercise), and lie supine on a ball in a neutral position. Once again, your partner can exert gentle pressure on the second ball by pushing away, pulling towards, pushing down or pulling up on the ball.

Pushing the ball to the left and right will exert considerable rotational force on your partner while pushing down on the ball stimulates the glutes to work even harder.

Progress to random changes of pressure on the ball - close your eyes and react!

SWAY STACK - PUSHING AWAY FROM PARTNER

PUSHING TO PARTNER'S RIGHT

SWAY STACK - PUSHING DOWN

Ski Stack

Both athletes assume a tuck position with the ball between them. Start to increase pressure through the ball in any combination of directions.

16 | The Maul

This is a free standing stack. You now have no external support to depend upon, so you must concentrate on sustaining a stable neutral posture, using the principles of upper and lower body power zones.

THE MAUL

As your partner exerts pressure on the ball, you should focus on bringing your stomach towards your spine, keeping your shoulders relaxed, and glutes working. Feel the muscles of your abdominal wall working as you resist the ball pressure.

17 | The Scrum

This exercise teaches you to use your gluteal and leg muscles to generate forward pressure.

Assume a position in which the ball is resting across the shoulder and upper arm. Find a comfortable position for your feet, and bring your trunk into a neutral position. Bring your stomach in, and focus on pushing through your feet, keeping the pelvis and shoulders pointing straight ahead. Increase the pressure against your partner, and imagine your line of force moving forward.

THE SCRUM

18 | The Linked Sway

Both athletes assume a sway position facing in opposite directions, and link arms. Maintaining a good neutral hip and back position, one athlete will pull against the other, challenging them to activate their abdominals and gluteals to resist the force. Hold for a count of 10 and swap roles.

THE LINKED SWAY

Connect Four Exercises

The aim of the Connect Four group of exercises is to introduce push and pull movements from a stable and neutral position with four points on one ball i.e. two arms and two legs or four arms. An important factor to consider during these exercises is the relative body weights of the partners. As with all Double Trouble exercises, the principles are communication, form and pacing.

19 | The Push Press

Assume a position where one partner lies on the floor with knees bent, and holds the ball while the other partner begins with the push-up start position.

From the start position, you and your partner have several options. One option is for the upper partner to perform a push-up, relying on the lower partner to stabilise the ball as the force increases during the lowering phase of the push-up. Simply reverse roles to challenge the lower partner to perform a push-up.

START POSITION FOR PUSH PRESS (FRONT)

UPPER PARTNER PUSH-UP

LOWER PARTNER PUSH-UP

20 | The Leg Press

One partner now lies on the floor while the other partner places the ball on his or her feet, and then takes up the push-up position as in the Push Press, with knees and hips straight, stomach pulled up towards the spine, and shoulder blades on the rib cage.

LEG PRESS START POSITION

The floor partner may perform a series of leg presses, concentrating on using the glutes to stabilise the legs. After 5-10 repetitions, the pressing partner may hold a position midway through the leg press range, to allow the other partner to perform push-ups.

Alternatively, this position can be used to let the upper partner perform a Ramp, as featured on page 74. Progress to performing these exercises with one leg.

THE LEG PRESS

21 | Kneeling Palm Press

Start with the ball at arms length and palms on the ball, making sure that your backs are flat and the shoulders are down.

Follow the same principles as during the Push Press, and attempt to perform push-ups using the ball as a focal point.

THE KNEELING PALM PRESS START POSITION

THE KNEELING PALM PRESS

22 | The Reactor

This exercise trains quick reactions from your leg, ankle and foot muscles and good body balance.

Sit on the ball with one foot on the ground and a partner holding your other foot. Bring your abdominals up and in.

You are primarily going to work the leg which is linked to the floor. Slightly tighten the muscles of the leg held by your partner so that it can be used to shift your body weight. Your partner will push through your foot to make the ball move forwards and backwards, side to side and at any angle. Begin slowly in small movements, and gradually increase the speed.

THE KNEELING PALM PRESS

111

SAMPLE SPORT SPECIIC PROGRAMMES

The following programmes are aimed at guiding you towards core exercises which address elements of a selection of sports. These lists should be regarded as samples only - every individual will have different needs and priorities, and you will find as you work through the book that there are other exercises which may suit your needs. These sample programmes are primarily to help you to problem solve for your sport, whether it is listed or not. By using a range of sports with different demands, we would like to assist you firstly to identify key movement requirements for your sport, and secondly exercises to address them.

In almost all of the sports mentioned, we have observed a strong tendency for the abdominal and gluteal muscles to work inadequately, and for the lower back muscles to work excessively. Many of the athletes who have presented to us with persistent back problems demonstrate this tendency, and it is not only associated with pain, but also loss of muscular efficiency. This should be borne in mind during all of the exercises, and extra care should be given to focusing on the target muscle to be worked, not just "going through the motions" using old poor muscular habits. If you are unsure how hard your back muscles are working, where possible feel the muscles with your fingers, or ask a training partner to monitor them : if there are big ridges of hard muscle either side of your spine, but your stomach is sagging and your "glutes" are soft, you know that you are not using the correct proportion of muscular effort. Remember - **form is everything.**

Swimming

- Trunk stabiliser strength and control in a streamlined position
- Balance between hip extensors and back extensors
- Coordinated pattern of upper and lower body stability

Programme:

Key exercises: 1- 5 at the appropriate level for your ability

First level additions:
(a) Sway: trains consistent ability to control a streamlined position
(b) Wall squat with arms above head in streamlined position

Second level additions:
(a) The Bodyspin - linear rotational control
(b) Titanic - higher load balance between back and hip extensors. NB this should only be done if the advanced superman has been mastered.

Skill Builders:
(a) 4-3-2 point balance

Double trouble:
(a) Standing double press
(b) Double ramp

Best weight training option:
(a) Pullover in suspension bridge position.

Ice Hockey

Demands of the sport:

- Multidirectional control
- Stability against external resistance
- Ability to generate explosive power
- Trunk rotation power and control

Programme:

Key exercises: 1-5 at appropriate level for your ability

First Level additions:
(a)   Ski shift - trains a stable trunk while transferring weight
(b)   Pendulum roll - trains rotational control through the trunk

Second Level additions:
(a)   Caterpillar - multidirectional trunk control
(b)   Ab burner - primary abdominal strength

Skill Builders:
(a)   Balance challenge - holding a medicine ball, keep your kneeling balance while turning your trunk to move the medicine ball from side to side.

(b)   The Wrestle

Double Trouble exercises:
(a)   The Maul
(b)   Single leg moving press

Best weight training option:
(a)   Single leg flyes in suspension bridge position

Netball

- explosive power, forward and upward
- speed with quick acceleration and deceleration
- agility
- ability to control rotational forces

Programme:

Key exercises: 1- 5 at the appropriate level for your ability

First level additions:

(a)   The Ham Sandwich - works hamstrings in both a lengthening and shortening action on a stable pelvis to address deceleration

(b)   The Windmill - trains the "glutes" to maintain a stable position for the hip and lower back, and the abdominals to create and control trunk rotation for strong accurate passing

Second level additions:

(a)   The Bodyspin - high level rotational control maintaining a neutral spine

Skill Builders:

(a)   Balance challenge
(b)   Slap hands
(c)   Sports specific passing
(d)   The Mogul Squat

Double trouble:

(a)   Double Ramp
(b)   Single Leg Hip Lift
(c)   Reactor

Best weight training option:

(a)   Cross body pullover, aiming to control trunk rotation through large resisted ranges of motion with the arms

Sprinting

- ability to maintain pelvic stability against large forces generated by the leg muscles
- explosive speed
- sustained efficient linear motion

Programme:

Key exercises:
1- 5 at the level appropriate for your ability. Pay particular attention to attaining high level progressions in the Superman, to increase the abdominal control of your pelvis and trunk and enhance the activity of your "glutes".

First Level additions:
(a)   The Ham Sandwich - trains pelvis to remain stable while stress is applied by the legs

(b)   The Ab Burner - beginning on knees, to train trunk control and high level abdominal strength

Second Level additions:
(a)   The Squat Ball Thrust - trains lumbo-pelvic control against leg movement

(b)   The Kickout (very high level) - integrates the entire body in linear motion with greater strength component

(c)   The Pullover (very high level) - integrates the whole body in linear motion with greater coordination and balance component

Skill Builders:
(a)   The Sprinter
(b)   Ballistic pushups

Double Trouble:
(a)   Single Leg Trunk Controller
(b)   Double Pump

Best weight training option:
(a)   weighted wall squat

Golf

- ability to sustain a neutral spinal position throughout a large range of motion
- ability to control rotation throughout the body
- strong support combined with mobility in the lower limbs

Programme:

Key exercises: (a) 1-5 at appropriate level for your abilities.

First level additions:
(a)   Around the World - trains rotational control with a neutral spine position (abdominal bias)
(b)   The Pendulum Roll - Rotational control with a gluteal bias

Second level additions:
(a)   The Bodyspin - requires rotational ability with hip mobility
(b)   The Windmill - trains rotation of the thorax on a stable lumbopelvic region

Skill Builders:
(a)   Balance challenge
(b)   The Twisting Spring

Double Trouble:
(a)   Double Hip Lift
(b)   The Stacks
(c)   The Maul

Best weight training option:
(a)   cross body pullover

Skiing

- sustained strength from the lower limbs
- ability to absorb changes in ski angle through lower limbs
- balance and quick reactions through trunk

Programme:

Key exercises:

1-5 as appropriate to your level of ability

First level additions:

(a) The Sway - trains gluteal endurance and trunk stability
(b) The Hamstring Pull - trains gluteal strength and holding ability and hamstring strength through shortening and lengthening actions.

Second level additions:

(a) The Caterpillar - whole body stability in a variety of directions
(b) The Ab Burner - advanced abdominal strengthening

Skill builders:

(a) The Twisting Spring
(b) 4-3-2 point balance
(c) The Mogul Squat

Double Trouble:

(a) The Stacks
(b) The Leg Press
(c) The Double Leg Squat

Best weight training option:

(a) The weighted wall squat/ cropped range lunge

Cricket

Demands of the sport:

- rotational control
- speed and agility
- ability to control large body displacements

Programme:

Key exercises:
1-5 as appropriate to your level of ability

First level additions:
(a)   The Pendulum Roll - introduces rotational stresses in supine (body facing upwards)
(b)   The Sway - trains gluteal endurance and trunk stability in lateral movements

Second level additions:
(a)   The Ramp - multidirectional stability for the shoulders arms and trunk
(b)   The Pullover - very high level whole body exercise using large range of arm and leg motion

Skill Builders:
(a)   4-3-2 Point Balance
(b)   The Wrestle
(c)   Walk the Walk
(d)   Slap Hands

Double Trouble:
(a)   The Stacks
(b)   The Maul
(c)   Standing Single Arm Press

Best weights option:
(a)   Batting - cross body pull, fast/medium bowling - outer range trunk lift

Martial Arts

- ability to maintain a neutral spinal position while rotating the thorax and using arms against resistance
- ability to retain control in the upper and lower power zones under random conditions (as speed and direction of opponents will vary)
- ability to control lateral and diagonal movements, maintaining a balanced base
- ability to control weapons, as the increased leverage of a long weapon elevates the demand for excellent spinal and hip positioning, with gluteal and abdominal muscles providing primary support.

Programme:

Key exercises

(a)   1-5 at appropriate level

First level additions:

(a)   The Pendulum Roll - teaches rotational control with gluteal endurance

(b)   Single Hand Wall Pushup - teaches scapular control, by learning to focus upper limb effort into the upper power zone

Second level additions:

(a)   Around The World - trains rotational control with abdominal and gluteal endurance

(b)   The Ramp - trains trunk and upper limb stability

Skill Builders:

(a)   Balance challenge

(b)   4-3-2 Point balance

Double Trouble:

(a)   Moving Press

(b)   The Stacks

(c)   The Maul

Best weight training option: (a) Pendulum Roll with one dumbell

FLEXIBILITY DEVELOPMENT AND STRETCHING WITH YOUR SWISS BALL

The objective of a stretch is to lengthen a muscle. This is important to maintain the range of motion of the joint that the muscle acts upon, to improve the muscle's function, and to prevent injury.

The stretches described in this section should be performed in a smooth, relaxed manner. Resist the urge to "bounce" at the end of range - this decreases the level of control you have, and tends to make the muscle reflexively shorten.

Each stretch is sustained for the count of 15-30 seconds, and can be performed 2-3 times.

1 | Neck Stretch

Sit "tall" on the ball, with fingertips touching the sides. Without bending at the trunk, slide the fingertips of one hand slightly down the ball, so that one shoulder is slightly lower than the other. Now bend your neck towards the other ear, feeling a gentle stretch down the side of the neck.

Note that the head has not turned, but is looking straight ahead. Hold. Repeat the exercise with the hand reaching down the other side of the ball. Remember, maintain neutral alignment. Maintaining the position of your shoulders and neck, turn your head to look towards the armpit. Hold. Swap sides.

2 | Lat Stretch

Sit "tall" on the ball, hands over head, with one hand grasping the wrist of the other. Reach upwards towards the ceiling on the side of the grasped wrist. Now pull the arm to the opposite side, to feel a stretch down the side of the trunk. If you do the upward reach first, you should not have to bend your trunk much to achieve a stretch. Hold.

3 | Tricep Stretch

Sit "tall" on the ball, and reach with the hand to touch the back of the shoulder of the same side. Make sure that the shoulder itself is relaxed i.e. not squeezed up towards the ear.

Apply gentle pressure at the elbow with the other hand, in a straight backwards direction. Hold.

4 | Hamstring Stretch

Sit on the ball with one leg slightly bent.
Roll the ball backwards, so that the back straightens upwards and the pelvis rolls forwards. Hold.

5 | Adductor Stretch

Sit on the ball with one leg out to the side. Roll the ball away from the straight leg, and slightly forward to feel an inner thigh stretch. Hold.

6 | Quad Stretch

Stand on one leg, holding an ankle. Make sure thighs stay together. Now tighten the lower abdominals and the gluteal (bottom) muscles, so that the front of the hip straightens. Hold.

Do not let your lower back "give" into a curve - it makes the stretch less focused, and increases the stress on the lower back.

7 | Hip Stretch

Place the ball against the wall, or, for more stability, in a corner. Rest a leg on the ball so that the knee falls outward, and "sit" in this position.

Keeping the chest up, lean forward to stretch the hip. Hold.

8 | Side Stretch

Kneel side-on to the ball. Straightening the outer leg and reaching with the uppermost arm, stretch across the ball sideways until you find the position which suits you best. You may find that straightening the inner leg stretches more effectively. Hold.

FULL SIDE STRETCH

9 | Pectoral Stretch

On hands and knees, rest one forearm on the ball so that the angle of you shoulder is about 90 degrees to your trunk. Gently allow the supported shoulder to sink towards the floor, so that the chest faces slightly away from the ball. At this point you should feel a stretch across your chest.

Keeping the chest facing away from the ball, roll it slightly upwards away from the body, so that your upper arm is slightly closer to your head. Find the position which best stretches you, and hold.

10 | Crossed Arm Stretch

Kneel behind the ball with hands crossed on the top of the ball. Sit back onto your feet so that your arms are now outstretched.

Roll the ball to one side until a stretch is felt under the upper arm and side of the trunk.

CROSSED ARM STRETCH TO THE LEFT

Repeat the stretch to the other side....

CROSSED ARM STRETCH TO THE RIGHT

11 | Extension Stretch

Begin from a half squat position with your back resting against the ball. Walk the feet away from the ball a step or two and roll backwards over the ball with arms overhead. Kneel behind the ball with hands crossed on the top of the ball. Sit back onto your feet so that your arms are now outstretched.

EXTENSION STRETCH

Elements of The Core Workout can be very beneficial as part of a pre-game or pre-event warm-up. Optimal performance is dependent on the body's neuromuscular system being primed, and a brief period of demand on an unstable apparatus such as the exercise ball can effectively facilitate this. It is best incorporated after the basic warm-up and stretches have been done, and should take no longer than 5-7 minutes. The exercises should be done with excellent form, and must be done with the aim of stimulating muscular firing. THEY MUST NOT BE PERFORMED TO FATIGUE.

The recommended individual pre-event exercises are:

- An appropriate level of balance challenge to "wake up" your system
- Suspension bridge
- Handspring
- Over the Top

WEIGHT TRAINING WITH YOUR SWISS BALL

Throughout the Core Workout, we have used the Swiss ball as
the primary tool for stability training. It can, however, be used to
complement other forms of training, such as working with weights,
and this concept is gaining popularity amongst trainers and sportspeople.
For this reason, we will briefly discuss the use of exercise balls in weight
training to introduce you to how they may be utilised in your programme.
However, it is not the objective of this manual to focus on weight training,
and we therefore stress that this is simply an introduction.

Why use exercise balls for weight training?

There are several advantages to using the ball when weight training.
One is the ability to make subtle changes to the angle of your effort when
lifting. This may allow you to target the range in which you need to work
your muscle most. Another is that you can monitor how effectively your
body can control a moving weight, as loss of control and compensatory
trunk movements will reflect in ball movement. Finally, using the ball while
lifting weights stimulates your stabilising muscles to react to limb loading,
which increases functional carryover from training into sports.

How do I incorporate the ball into weight training?

Firstly, the principles which you have learned throughout the Core Workout
will have laid good foundations for your weight training. The concepts of
neutral alignment, stomach flattening, breathing and power zones should
apply in the same ways to weight training as for core stability work, and
often injuries or poor outcomes are results of being unaware of their
importance. Remember that you are aiming for the most efficient, most
effective and safest methods of training to gain optimal results.

The next thing to bear in mind is that weight training with good form on the ball increases the demand on your neuromuscular system, due to the increased activity required of your stabilising muscles. You will find that your ability to maintain excellent form is dependent on your level of fatigue, and that you may initially fatigue more quickly due to the higher muscular activity and concentration required to perform the exercises correctly. Adequate recovery time is therefore necessary between sets, as fatigue and decreased coordination are closely correlated, and will lead to compensatory strategies from the body and a loss of efficiency. You may find that your neuromuscular endurance varies from session to session, but by monitoring your body's response and adjusting your rest periods accordingly you will make the most of your effort. ***Remember: Form is Everything.*** Training for optimal muscular activity in this manner has excellent potential for carryover into sporting activity, as performance on the field, track or court is highly dependent on endurance not only of single groups of muscles, but also of the body's ability to repeatedly reproduce a set of skills which depend on complex muscular interactions over time.

When beginning to work with the ball, it is advisable that you use a lower load, higher repetition strategy. It takes practice to adjust to the relative instability of the ball as a support surface, and you need to give yourself time to learn the new muscular patterns which will be necessary. This will be safer if you use a less heavy weight. For this reason, we suggest that you introduce only a couple of exercises using the ball at a time, so that it does not disrupt your regular programme too much, or tempt you to try weights that you cannot control adequately.

Two or three Core Exercises exercises performed during a warm-up can help to stimulate the body's neuromuscular system prior to a workout, but these must not be done to fatigue. The idea is to prime the body for exercise, not put it at a disadvantage by tiring the mechanisms which will make your workout more effective. For similar reasons, after a warm-up the most challenging exercises should be performed first while fatigue has less influence, and less demanding exercises performed as the programme progresses.

Safety Tips

- Do not use foot weights during any of the exercises. You are trying to train your trunk stabilisers to act as your 'anchor', and fixed feet will stimulate the wrong muscle pattern.

- Always use a spotter, particularly during movements such as incline bench press where the ball may slip backwards. You may also use a wall to support the ball.

- Select lighter weights when using the ball due to the increased neuromuscular demand and increased whole body muscle activity.

Examples of ball use for weight training

The ball can be used as an alternative multi-angled bench

The Bench Press

Those who perform this exercise regularly often try to vary the angle of effort in order to work slightly different parts of the chest muscle and anterior shoulder. Conventional benches can limit the potential for this, but the ball allows very subtle variations.

Notice that the skills which you learned in the suspension bridge are necessary here. Abdominals and gluteals need to work, and special attention must be paid to not using the lower back muscles for support. If this is difficult, try tipping the pelvis slightly back towards you.

When varying the angle of effort, be careful to keep the neck and lower back in neutral.

It is vital that you use a spotter during all exercises, particularly when using the ball as a bench. You may also wish to use a wall to support the ball and prevent it from shooting out from under you.

STANDARD BENCH PRESS ON THE BALL

INCLINE BENCH PRESS ON THE BALL

133

The same idea can be applied to bias muscle groups in slightly different ways. For example, the suspension bridge position is used to work 'lats' and long head of tricep, and with a shift of position triceps and deltoid (shoulder) muscles are working. In this way the tricep group has been worked fully in terms of range, action, and its role in terms of its functional relationship with other muscle groups.

START POSITION

FINISH POSITION

ALTERNATIVE START POSITION

FINISH POSITION

An alternative way to use the ball is for monitoring body balance, incorrect use of momentum, and compensatory body sway.

The Bicep Curl

Sit on the ball, as you would on a bench in standard dumbell curls. Begin by lengthening your spine from the back part of the top of your head, allowing your stomach to fall in and your shoulders to settle down and back. Stabilise your scapula by flattening it onto your rib cage, and keep it from rolling up and forward.

BICEP CURL START POSITION

BICEP CURL ON THE BALL

Now proceed with the bicep curl, but use your abdominal muscles to limit the amount that your trunk moves on the ball. You are aiming for *almost no ball movement.* The same principle applies to the vertical and lateral raise.

VERTICAL RAISE ON THE BALL

LATERAL RAISE ON THE BALL

Cross-body patterns with Resistance

It is important to practice this movement without a weight initially, so that you become familiar with the muscle patterns necessary to control the rotational movement, and when introducing weight, to begin with very small amounts. For example, when we introduced this exercise to a group of international rugby players in their late teens, a weight of 2 kgs was more than sufficient to work them hard. You may need to start with as little as 500 grams in some cases - remember that this exercise demands that the trunk and arms control large ranges of motion, and small weights can generate large forces at the extremes of range.

Assume a suspension bridge position. Flatten your stomach by pulling up and in with the abdominal muscles, and make sure your buttocks are working to support you. If you feel that your lower back is working more than your glutes, lower your hips slightly and tip your pelvis back towards you to relax the back muscles. The hips must remain level at all times during the motion, and the head and neck in neutral. Try to visualise keeping a "long neck".

Grasping the weight in both hands, begin with the arms straight up towards the ceiling. Keeping firm control with your abdominals, move the weight slightly to one side and above your head, in a slow arc. Your trunk will want to arch upwards and twist, but this must be controlled by your abdominal muscles.

CROSS BODY MOVEMENT TO THE LEFT

When you reach a comfortable limit with your arms, stabilise firmly with the abdominals and bring the weight slowly over to the hips on the opposite side of your body.
Repeat 4-10 times, and then repeat the movement beginning on the opposite side.

CROSS BODY MOVEMENT TO THE RIGHT

Wall Ball Squat

Using either a barbell across the shoulders or dumbells in your hands, you are able to add resistance to the basic wall squat.

Assume a position as for the Wall Squat. Make sure that your feet are far enough forward to prevent your knee from moving beyond them at the lowest point in your squat. Focus on keeping your spine in a neutral position by scooping your abdominals up and in, and generate support for your pelvis by squeezing your glutes. Keeping the knees in line with the ankles, slowly roll down, to a point where your knees make an angle no less than 90 degrees. Keeping the stomach in, push up again slowly, focusing on pushing from the glutes.

WALL BALL SQUAT WITH DUMBELLS

You also have the option of raising the dumbells to shoulder height, and with a barbell, positioning the load in front (front squat position) or behind you (back squat).

Cropped Range Lunge

Start with the ball against the wall and one foot on the ball. Using a low weight at either waist or shoulder height, bend the front knee through a range of motion which can be controlled with the foot flat and the body in neutral alignment. To perform this exercise well, you will need good abdominal support and well activated gluteals.

START POSITION

CROPPED RANGE LUNGE

You can increase the demands of this exercise by using the ball off the wall. Furthermore, some people prefer to move the ball slightly back as they lunge, and bring the ball back to the start position between each repetition.

The ball can also be used for prone support, to make some standard exercises much safer.

Reverse Fly

In the reverse fly, it is common to assume a start position which puts the back in a relatively unsafe posture. By using the ball, your chest is supported, taking the strain off the lower back and focusing your efforts into your midback, as is the intended purpose of the exercise. Remember that the same guidelines apply as for every other exercise -abdominals pulled towards the spine, neck in neutral, and shoulder blades away from the ears and flat on the rib cage.

Superman

Similarly, the same technique can be used for the lower traps, but it must be stressed that you should be able to perform the Superman exercise well before weight is applied to the movement. The most common error is to let the shoulder blade creep up towards your ear as your arm raises.

For most of us, the abdominals are more than adequately trained in relatively small ranges of movement. As we have explored throughout the Core Workout, the deep muscles of the abdominal wall which are responsible for stability are those most often missed in training, and it is these that we have fundamentally concentrated on. For some athletes, however, the abdominals responsible for movement play a crucial role in their sport, and in much more vulnerable and demanding positions. For example *javelin throwers, fast bowlers and gymnasts* need to be able to use the different actions of the abdominal muscles to superimpose a movement role over a stabilising role. For athletes such as these, the ball is ideal to reproduce positions of vulnerability and allow quite specific training. To perform such a movement, the "tran abs" must be activated first, pulling the stomach in towards the spine, and as the trunk curls up, the focus must be on keeping the stomach flat.

Outer range trunk lift

This is a high level abdominal exercise, and is only recommended for well-conditioned athletes for whom outer range abdominal control is relevant. It is essential that you have developed good strength and stability in your 'trans abs' by practising a range of the core exercises such as Over The Top, The Ab Burner and the Body Spin prior to attempting this exercise, which demands a combination of movement and stabilisation from the abdominals.

It is important that you master your technique prior to introducing an external weight i.e. dumbell. Assume a position on the ball where by the upper part of your trunk is slightly arched backward. Do not go too far to begin with, as this will be an unfamiliar range to control at first.

Your "anchor" will be provided by your trans abs, so it is not advisable to fix your feet under a weight, or to have someone hold your feet down for you. Begin with the stomach flattening, then gently exhale and imagine your ribs pulling towards your pelvis. Keep your chin tucked in as your shoulders raise to just above level with your hips. Keep focusing on stomach flattening as you lower back down again.

This exercise can also be done on a slight diagonal, by beginning with one elbow pointing down towards the floor, and finishing with that same elbow pointing across the opposite hip.

It must be reinforced that in order to perform these exercises correctly, a great deal of core stability is necessary. They in no way replace other core exercises, but offer a sports specific option to those athletes who require strength in greater range than normal.

These are only a few examples of how the exercise ball can be used for weight training, but by reviewing the principles above, you may find that the ball can enhance your normal programme and improve the way in which your body responds to external loading.

BIBLIOGRAPHY

Bartonietz,K and Strange,D. (1998) "The Use Of Swiss Balls In Athletic Training - An Effective Combination Of Load And Fun". IAAF Quarterly No. 2/ pp35-41

Bullock-Saxton, J., Janda,V., Bullock,M. (1993) Reflex Activation Of Gluteal Muscles In Walking. An approach To Restoration Of Muscle Function For Patients With Low Back Pain. Spine 18(6): 704-8.

Carriere, B. "Swiss Ball Exercises". PT Magazine, September 1993

Foxhoven, B. and Plate, P.(1996) "Athletes With Back Pain - A Trunk Stabilisation Program". Strength and Conditioning Journal Aug pp 69 - 73

Gracovetsky,S A . (1997) "Linking The Spinal Engine With The Legs: A Theory Of Human Gait" in Vleeming,A., Mooney,V., Dorman,T., Snijders,C., Stoeckart,R. (1997) Movement, Stability and Low Back Pain - the essential role of the pelvis. Churchill Livingstone:London.

Kapandji,I.A.(1982) The Physiology Of The Joints Vols I, II and III. Churchill Livingston:London

Lee,D. (1997) "Instability of the Sacroiliac Joint and the Consequences Of Gait" in Vleeming,A., Mooney,V., Dorman,T., Snijders,C., Stoeckart,R. (1997) Movement, Stability and Low Back Pain - the essential role of the pelvis. Churchill Livingstone:London.

Lippincott, Williams and Wilkins. (1999) First Randomized Trial Of Treatments For Groin Pain" Sports Medicine Digest 21 (3):25-30.

Mottram, S. and Comerford, M.(1998) "Stability, Dysfunction and Low Back Pain". Journal of Orthopedic Medicine 20(2) :13 -18.

Norris, C. M. (1994)"Abdominal Training: Dangers And Exercise Modifications". Physiotherapy in Sport 19 ;5 :10 -13

Richardson, CA and Jull,GA (1994) "Concepts of Assessment and Rehabilitation for Active Lumbar Stability" in Boyling,J and Palastanga, N. Grieve's Modern Manual Therapy. Churchill Livingstone: London.

Richardson, C.A and Jull, G.A. (1995) "Muscle Control - Pain Control. What Exercises Would You Prescribe?". Manual Therapy 1: 1-9.

CONTACT INFORMATION

For further information regarding The Core Workout, courses, updates and other products including Fitballs, please contact either Joanne or Paul. If you have any questions regarding the exercises or workouts specific to your sport, please do not hesitate to contact us.

Paul T Pook

Fitness 4 Sport LLP
32 Turners Avenue
Fleet
Hampshire GU51 1DX
Tel: 01252 816666
www.fitness4rugby.com
e-mail: paul@fitness4rugby.com

Joanne Elphinston

Elphinston Human Performance
Askrigg
Leckwith Road
Llandough
Vale of Glamorgan
Cardiff
CF64 2LY
e-mail: jelphinston@yahoo.com